Presented To:

_____

From:

_____

Date:

_____

DESTINY IMAGE BOOKS BY BOB LARSON

Demon-Proofing Prayers

Curse Breaking

FREEDOM FROM THE BONDAGE OF GENERATIONAL SIN

BOB LARSON

DESTINY IMAGE® PUBLISHERS, INC.

P.O. Box 310, Shippensburg, PA 17257-0310

"Promoting Inspired Lives."

This book and all other Destiny Image, Revival Press, MercyPlace, Fresh Bread, Destiny Image Fiction, and Treasure House books are available at Christian bookstores and distributors worldwide.

For a U.S. bookstore nearest you, call 1-800-722-6774.

For more information on foreign distributors, call 717-532-3040.

Reach us on the Internet: www.destinyimage.com.

ISBN 13 TP: 978-0-7684-0329-9

ISBN 13 Ebook: 978-0-7684-8571-4

For Worldwide Distribution, Printed in the U.S.A.

11 12 13 / 22 21 20 19

DEDICATION

This book is dedicated to my incredible wife and three precious daughters.

In addition to Holy Scripture, the information in this book is the result of my ministry to many thousands of people. What I've learned from these real-life encounters with brokenhearted individuals has confirmed many times over the reality of devastating, generational curses. It is the gracious understanding of my family that permits me to be gone for these extended times of ministry. Countless lives have been changed and many diabolic curses broken because my family made the sacrifice that permitted me to help others all over the world.

For this reason, and for their persevering love for me and the Lord, I dedicate this book to them.

ACKNOWLEDGMENTS

The understanding of how generational curses operate has required a lifetime of Bible study as well as direct experience with the victims of such curses. My files contain many thousands of case studies that confirm in detail how these curses operate. I want to acknowledge the importance of those who have opened up their lives to the possibility of receiving this important ministry. These unsung heroes have spared no details to discover how the devil operated in their lives. As a result, they were set free from these debilitating curses, and I was able to more fully comprehend the evil web that Satan weaves, generation after generation.

I also want to acknowledge the many dedicated members of our DWJD® (Do What Jesus Did) healing and deliverance teams all around the world. Their determination to set the captives free has uncovered many previously unknown devices of the devil in this spiritual arena of curses. I am thankful to be surrounded by so many dedicated men and women of God who selflessly labor to free all those bound by the evil of their ancestors.

CONTENTS

PRACTICAL RESOURCES TO BREAK CURSES

CURSES AREN'T BROKEN UNTIL THEY'RE BROKEN

A good-looking, genial young man was waiting in the lobby for me. I introduced myself, and we made our way to my office. The minute we stepped inside, things started happening—unusual jerks, twists, and movements.

"Where did you pick up these tics?" I asked.

"They're not really tics," he said. "They feel like jolts, and they affect me only when I am praying, reading my Bible, or when I am around spiritual things. The rest of the time I don't have these manifestations."

He had come to me after some successful ministry from one of our trained and chartered DWJD (Do What Jesus Did) healing and deliverance teams. He sought out their help, and they had broken many curses already, leaving me with only the final curses to mop up. But the other team had not been able to crack the code, so to speak. Neither they nor the young man himself had been able to determine what to do next, although their time together had effectively paved the way for what happened that day in my office.

The rough outline of his life was this: When he was a young child, his father had died. His mother became preoccupied with her romantic pursuits and other things, and he felt abandoned. Eventually his mother remarried, but his stepfather did not treat him in a healthy way. As the boy's life deteriorated, he started having dreams in which he saw demons.

Curse Breaking

The two primary demons that he saw called themselves Hate and Blasphemy. Not knowing what to do, he visited a couple of Native American witchdoctors. Instead of solving his problem, they worsened it because instead of getting rid of demons, he got more of them. And yet his problem seemed to be more deeply rooted than these circumstances could account for.

My team and I prayed with him at some length. Finally, I felt the Lord was suggesting that we have him take communion. As it turned out, he could hardly swallow, holding the elements in his mouth for a while and fighting to get them down. The moment he swallowed, more manifestations started. In fact, the primary evil spirit that was provoking the manifestations spoke out through the young man's voice, calling itself the Ancient of Ancients and declaring, "He belongs to us."

As we began to trace what had happened in the past, I demanded to know how many generations the curse went back, starting out with two, four, and six generations. Even when we reached 24 generations, I didn't feel we were getting the right answer. Finally we settled on 34 generations. Whether a generation is figured according to the biblical model of Israel's wandering (40 years) or the modern model of generational replication (18 to 22 years), this curse went back a long time—somewhere between 600 and 1300 years.

We interrogated the demon to find out what had happened 34 generations ago. The demon bragged, "I killed them all, women and children. I am Murder." So some kind of bloodshed had happened to this man's ancestors. Eventually we uncovered the fact that this happened in Spain. In fact, the young man began to speak in Spanish (which he had not studied). I brought my assistant into the room because she is Puerto Rican, and she translated for us. The murders had happened at the hands of a Spanish soldier who was possessed by spirits of Hate, Blasphemy, and Murder. This ancient soldier had killed a pregnant Christian woman along with her unborn baby. A fragment of consciousness of this unforgiven sin had been passed down through all those generations. By bringing the matter before God and issuing forgiveness, we were able to break the curse and cast out the demon once and for all.

(Someday I think I will write a book called Demons Say the Darndest Things, because so often they do. Just before this one was cast out, I remember him saying in an irritated voice, "You know, hope is a dangerous thing." He was referring to the hope that had carried this young man from one part of the country to another, seeking freedom from the demonic curse.)

The man walked out of my office very much changed. At last he was free. The curse of his Spanish ancestor who had committed murder was broken.

I share this true story because it illustrates many of the principles I will describe in this book. This young man's contemporary problems were the result of something that had happened 34 generations before. He had suffered a complete breakdown and had become psychotic for about four years. He had lost his marriage as well as his emotional and physical health.

And his is not an isolated case. Most of us, whether we realize it or not, have run into similar situations of great suffering that can be traced to some great evil that was committed a long time ago. Many have such unbroken curses in our own lives. This should not surprise us too much. After all, every one of us inherited the curse of original sin, descended as we are from Adam and Eve. Even after we break that curse through our relationship with Jesus Christ, the effect of that original sin on our ancestors may remain unresolved. Every single person has people in his or her past who committed great evils. Some renegade or pervert is perched on a branch of your family tree. You may not have to go back very far to find something; just show up at your next family reunion and look around.

You may be a good person, even one of the most Christ-centered people around. You may say, "Well, I think I am doing pretty well spiritually and emotionally." But we tend to gauge ourselves by how well we're doing, not by how well we might be doing. It is one of the fallacies of the Christian life. We judge ourselves by how well we're getting along, not by how much more we might do for the Lord or by how much more freedom we might enjoy. We settle for less than the best. Sometimes it takes a crisis to make us seek help.

My goal in this book is to open your eyes to possible additional sources of your intractable problems, whether they are dramatic and attention grabbing or simply "background noise" to which you have become accustomed. Do you suffer from endless ailments? Do you see troubled patterns in your relationships? Do fears plague you?

You have lived long enough to know the patterns of your impulses and sinful tendencies. By now, you may have identified some of the lies upon which you base your decisions and actions. You may have tried to overcome these vulnerabilities and liabilities through prayer, Bible-reading, and even counseling. And you may have discovered that nothing seems to work. You can stuff them and bluff your way past them for only so long. Sooner or later, you will realize that no amount of counseling or effort can banish certain evil thought patterns, physical ailments, or insecurities. Maybe it is time to consider how curses—both relatively recent ones as well as those of long-ago origin—are holding you captive.

Curses can be predicated on known events, but often we do not know what has happened to our families, especially if something occurred a long time before we were born. To find out what we are dealing with, we must rely on a combination of spiritual discernment and acquired knowledge of common sources for curses. Besides surrendering our lives as much as possible to the ultimate curse-breaker, Jesus Christ, we must educate ourselves about how curses work, biblically and historically, before we can achieve total victory over them.

In the chapters of this book, we will look at a number of causes for curses, from innocuous-seeming verbal statements to unusual experiences. My desire is to help you "crack the code" for your own life.

Do not be frightened when you recognize yourself in something you read in the following pages. Trust that God has brought it to your attention because He wants to open your eyes to your personal spiritual reality, and believe that He will bring you through to complete freedom. He is bigger than any sin and more powerful than any demon or curse, and He loves you. He always prepares the way before you. Know that you are not alone in your struggle; you can talk to sympathetic and experienced people (see the final section of the book for more information about my ministry), and they will know what to do.

Come with me now to learn what you need to know about curses.

Chapter 1

WHAT YOU NEED TO KNOW ABOUT CURSES

The year I entered kindergarten, my sister, who is my only sibling, graduated from high school. Essentially I was raised as an only child. My mother's German background gave her a cultural expectation that her children would take care of her in her old age, and that was part of the reason my parents waited so long to have another child. Here is how my father explained it when they were still alive:

"We had planned to have only one child. When your sister was born fourteen years before you, we thought that one child was enough. One night many years later, your mother and I were talking, and she was concerned about who would take care of her in her old age. That night, you were conceived."

Growing up, I heard this story every now and then, and I thought it was kind of heartwarming. I never thought much about it, except to recognize that I had been born to take care of my mother and be the person she wanted me to be.

Sure enough, in their old age, my parents had some financial problems and serious health issues. From the time I was in my early twenties until they died, I was their sole support. I bought their cars, paid the rent on their apartment, eventually bought them a townhouse, took care of their utilities, paid their bills, and more. I felt good about it. I patted myself on the back because I felt I was being an honorable child to look after my parents in this way.

I felt good about it until I reached a crisis point in mid-life and a dear friend asked me some tough questions. Suddenly that wonderful story had a flaw. What was wrong with that scenario? For my whole life up to that time, I had been saddled with a faulty sense of significance. I finally figured out that deep down I didn't feel I had been born because my parents loved each other, which they did, but instead because my mother wanted a son to look after her in her waning years. In other words, as a son, I represented only functional financial and emotional security for my mother and father. Although I never resented my role as their provider and we had a very pleasant relationship, I had no sense of personal significance apart from what I could do to help them. Someone who feels that way does not grow up with a sense of unconditional love. There are strings attached.

There is more. I am also one of the many people in the world whose parents never said, "I love you" outright, at least not until they were in their eighties and I was in my forties. When my friend asked me, "Do your parents love you?" I gave the stock answer:

"Of course they do."

Then he questioned, "Do they say so?"

"Well no, but I am sure they do." This good friend went to my parents and brought this issue—their lack of verbalizing love—to their attention. They had neglected the most important thing because of looking at me in such a utilitarian manner for so long. They were more than eager to correct their neglect. Every day for the rest of their lives when I spoke to them, they would tell me they loved me. My mother eventually developed dementia, so she was no longer communicative in her last years, but my father was lucid until the end. The last memory I have of my father is bending down to kiss his forehead and hearing his final words to me: "Son, I love you."

God brought it full circle. A big part of my life had been under the curse of feeling unloved, and none of us understood it. Once the curse was broken, healing came at last. Now I am free to continue to learn how to love and receive love.

A lot of things are like that. Situations that you do not see as particularly injurious or damaging can in fact seriously damage your life. It almost seems too heavy to call it a curse. But the Holy Spirit can show you what words or actions in the past have caused you to walk under the cloud of debilitating generational sins, and He can help you break free.

WHAT IS A CURSE?

Curses need to be considered from two perspectives: (1) implicit or unintentional curses such as the one I described above, and (2) explicit or intentional ones that are invoked specifically to bring evil upon a person, group of persons, or human agency. I will expand upon both types.

Implicit Curses

Most curses "just happen." That is not to imply that they are inconsequential, however. My definition of an implicit, unintentional curse is as follows:

> The inexorable (relentless), immutable (incapable of change) consequence of conduct and communication inherited transgenerationally, continuing until altered by spiritual intervention.

By "conduct and communication" I mean ordinary-seeming behavior and interactions between people, behavior that may not transgress any moral or civil law and that may not bring obvious damage. If somebody goes to a witch doctor and has him stick a needle into a voodoo doll, that is intentional act. It will result in an explicit curse. But if that same person, exasperated with some family member or associate, explodes and says, "You crazy idiot! Nobody will ever trust you again!" that could release an implicit curse that would interfere with the person's life for a long time.

Curses land not only on the person who is being cursed, but they also affect the person who does the cursing. This principle is in accord with Jesus's warning: "Judge not, that you be not judged" (Matt. 7:1). This is why human society consists of such a web of unintentional curses.

Whole families and ethnic groups carry implicit curses. The Irish really do have a problem with booze. Germans really do have an issue with wars (and as I just indicated, I am of German descent, so I know what I am talking about). Not only individuals and their families can perpetuate a curse, but also human groupings such as governments, institutions, denominations, and churches. The curse can affect the conduct of the corporate group and also its legacy.

Once curses have been uttered or created by any means, they go on and on. Curses are characterized by a certain doggedness. They do not change until spiritual intervention takes place. They can affect more than one generation and, therefore, more than one person in the long run, even if they were issued against a single individual in the first place.

Explicit Curses

Explicit curses can sometimes be easier to spot, because they originate from an intentional act. Here is my definition of an explicit curse:

> The malediction of evil invoked by ritual, ceremony, or incantation with directive intent to bring evil, misfortune, harm, or injury to individuals, families, institutions, or legacies.

However, if a curse originated a long time ago or if the cursed person considers the source to be innocuous or safe, explicit curses can be just as hard to discern as implicit ones. The key difference is that they are purposeful, often occurring in the context of a religious observance motivated by malice toward a perceived enemy.

A curse is a prayer—a prayer for injury or harm or misfortune to fall upon somebody. Noah pronounced a curse on Canaan (see Genesis 9:24-27). Isaac pronounced a curse on anyone who cursed Jacob (see Genesis 27:29). The soothsayer Balaam was hired by Balak, king of Moab, to pronounce a curse on the Israelites (see Numbers 22-24). Goliath, the Philistine giant of Gath, "cursed David by his gods" (1 Sam. 17:43).

In Bible times, a curse was considered to be more than a mere wish that evil would befall one's enemies. The words themselves were believed to possess the power to bring about the evil. Just as prayer has been defined as a wish referred to God, curses refer to the invocation of supernatural beings who have the power to inflict harm. In ancient times, a god, a deity, or some spiritual entity was always attached to a curse. This is more serious than the kinds of angry statements we hear often in our current culture, such as "God damn you" or "Go to hell."

When the ancients voiced a curse, they meant it, and they expected their supplication to be carried out by whatever supernatural being they were invoking. In fact, it was quite common for them to commit the curse to writing; they didn't think it was enough for them to merely utter it aloud, although a curse that is only uttered aloud will be effective. In Zechariah 5:1-3, the "flying scroll" with curses inscribed on both sides of it "goes out over the face of the whole earth" to find its way into the house of every thief and perjurer (those who steal or who make false statements under oath).

The various Hebrew nouns and verbs having to do with cursing were rendered differently depending on the degree of strength desired, but they are more or less synonymous. The bottom line is that the words of a curse declare the opposite of the words of a blessing and that both curses and blessings are more than mere wishes because their words have the power to carry out their intended meaning.

Both in ancient times and today, words of cursing and blessing issue forth from the human heart, as pure or as tainted as it may be: "A good man brings good things out of the good stored up in him, and an evil man brings evil things out of the evil stored up in him" (Matt. 12:35 NIV).

God Declares Curses

In the Garden, God Himself is described as cursing the serpent (see Genesis 3:14-15) as well as the ground (see Genesis 3:17). In the New Testament, we see Jesus cursing the fig tree that did not bear fruit, saying "Let no fruit grow on you ever again" (Matt. 21:19). And immediately the fig tree withered away (see also Mark 11:14). He also taught Christians how to deal with curses, saying: "Bless those who curse you..." (Luke 6:28).

Most of us are familiar with the curse found in Malachi 3, because some preacher will have quoted it when he is about to take up an offering:

*"Will a man rob God? Yet you have robbed Me! But you say,
'In what way have we robbed You?' In tithes and offerings.*

You are cursed with a curse, for you have robbed Me, even this whole nation. Bring all the tithes into the storehouse, that there may be food in My house, and try Me now in this," says the Lord of hosts, *"If I will not open for you the windows of heaven and pour out for you such blessing that there will not be room enough to receive it. And I will rebuke the devourer for your sakes, so that he will not destroy the fruit of your ground, nor shall the vine fail to bear fruit for you in the field,"* says the Lord of hosts (Malachi 3:8-11).

Here the prophet Malachi, speaking for God, makes it plain that when people withhold the blessing of their substance from God, they bring about a curse.

Interestingly, not all maladies that appear to be curses result in evil, at least in the long run. Consider the story of the man who was blind from birth, recounted in John 9:1-3:

Now as Jesus passed by, He saw a man who was blind from birth. And His disciples asked Him, saying, "Rabbi, who sinned, this man or his parents, that he was born blind?"Jesus answered, "Neither this man nor his parents sinned, but that the works of God should be revealed in him.

And He healed the man's blindness on the spot.

God's curses lead to justice and judgment, reformation and repentance. Instead of being destructive, they are warnings of consequence for disobedience. They can also lead to outright blessings. God spoke to Abraham and told him, "I will bless those who bless you, and I will curse him who curses you; and in you all the families of the earth shall be blessed" (Gen. 12:3).

Both God's curses and His blessings are conditional, as we see in the prophetic words of Moses:

Behold, I set before you today a blessing and a curse: the blessing, if you obey the commandments of the Lord your God which I command you today; and the curse, if you do not obey the commandments of the Lord your God, but turn aside from the way which I command you today, to go after other gods which you have not known (Deuteronomy 11:26-28).

The "Causeless Curse"

In spite of the inherent power of the words of a curse, the principle of cause and effect prevails. We learn this from the well-known proverb: "Like the sparrow in her wandering, like the swallow in her flying, so the causeless curse does not alight" (Prov. 26:2 AMP). The Living Bible puts it this way: "An undeserved curse has no effect. The intended victim of the curse will be no more harmed by an unmerited curse than by a bird flitting through the sky."

This does not mean, as many Christians seem to think, that believers are immune to all curses. It means that the devil can only activate curses based on true causes and that maledictions cannot land on people just because their enemies hate them. Still, unfair as it may seem, some curse-causes are beyond our initial control because they occurred to our ancestors or to the members of a group to which we belong.

Satan looks for a cause. He will pin the curse on some current event in the person's life, if he can find one. But more often he will find a cause in a previous generation, and he'll use that to bring the curse to life, particularly if he can link the long-ago cause to a present-day action. He wants to set curses in motion because he wants to bring more disease, death, and destruction upon all humanity. That's his MO.

My premise is that we all suffer from curses to a greater or lesser degree. With the sinful accumulation of centuries behind us, the only thing keeping most of us from living devastated lives is that we have not had the life experiences in the here and now that would have given substance to an ancient curse, reigniting it and giving it the right to land on us. Almost always, a current event triggers an ancient curse that would otherwise be causeless. Take sexual violation as a case in point. If today someone gets raped, molested, or otherwise sexually violated, ancient curses can suddenly come to life.

CHRIST, CURSED FOR YOU AND ME

The Bible tells us clearly that Jesus Christ was made a curse for us. People who do not like to hear a message such as mine often choose to quote Paul's words: "Christ has redeemed us from the curse of the law, having become a curse for us (for it is written, 'Cursed is everyone who hangs on a tree')" (Gal. 3:13, quoting Deut. 21:23). They consider Christ's sacrifice on the cross to be the blanket solution to all curses, and they say that everything related to curse breaking is a bunch of bunk.

Such people confuse positional truth with conditional reality. The positional truth is that, yes, Jesus Christ was cursed for us, and yes, He bore the curse of sin to the cross, and yes, because of His resurrection victory over death, we ought to be free from every curse. But like every promise in the Word of God, this one is of no effect until you believe it, receive it, and appropriate it by faith. The Good News is powerful. The bad news is that it is not automatic. Each person needs to appropriate the blessing of salvation as it applies to the realities of his or her own life.

HOW CURSES WORK

We have already touched on the fact that curses are often hereditary, involuntary, and transgenerational. In other words, they can be transferred geographically and historically over time, sometimes a very long time. The classic Scriptures about this include the following:

You shall have no other gods before Me. You shall not make for yourself a carved image—any likeness of anything that is in heaven above, or that is in the earth beneath, or that is in the water under the earth; you shall not bow down to them nor serve them. For I, the Lord your God, am a jealous God, visiting the iniquity of the fathers upon the children to the third and fourth generations of those who hate Me (Exodus 20:3-5).

And the Lord passed before him [Moses] and proclaimed, "The Lord, the Lord God, merciful and gracious, longsuffering, and abounding in goodness and truth, keeping mercy for thousands, forgiving iniquity and transgression and sin, by no means clearing the guilty, visiting the iniquity of the fathers upon the children and the children's children to the third and the fourth generation" (Exodus 34:6-7).

The third and fourth generations was not meant to be taken literally, except as a minimum. The writer indicates that a curse can follow a family or national line for at least four generations, but he doesn't put an end on it there. Essentially, he indicates that a curse remains active in perpetuity, although as I have already said, it may or may not remain activated.

The same principle applies to blessings; they too follow to the third and fourth generation and beyond. Most of us would be eager to accept blessings from our ancestors, wouldn't we? We object to the idea of inheriting curses, but we are quite happy to receive the cosmic justice of blessings.

Moral choice matters. Something has to happen to activate both curses and blessings in the present time. If they do not have a reason to land on you, essentially they remain dormant and ineffective. You could say that, where a godly person is concerned, old curses may be in a kind of remission. Or they may remain in abeyance for someone because of the godliness of an ancestor. When something comes along to ignite them, we need to know how they work and what to do about them. You and I, living in the endtimes, get to be part of the ultimate resolution of the evil of the ages. We can break the curses that come from antiquity, from the iniquities of our ancestors, as we prepare a "radiant church, without stain or wrinkle or any other blemish, but holy and blameless" (Eph. 5:27 NIV).

THE CONTINUITY AND ADAPTABILITY OF CURSES

Curses have continuity, and they remain unbroken until they get broken in the right way. I usually put it this way: "A curse isn't broken until it's broken." Invoked in perpetuity, curses do not just die of natural causes.

One of the reasons curses have such longevity is because they are adaptable. Sometimes they leapfrog over an entire generation, most often because it is a godly one. Let's say you're trying to find out if someone's problem is the result of a generational curse, so you start asking the person about their family. You say, "What was your father like?"

"Daddy was a preacher man, a good man. Grandpa was, too. So was his daddy and his daddy's grandpa. As far back as I can trace, everybody has been a Christian and a good person."

Why, then, is this person so miserable? Something has come back to life that seems to have been lying dormant for a long time. It is like a disease. Inheritable diseases do not necessarily transmit to the very next generation, do they? When you walk into a doctor's office, he wants to know about your medical history and your family medical history. You fill out those long forms for him. Essentially the diseases listed on his forms are generational curses. The doctor wants to know who had what disease and who died of what malady because it can give him clues about what's ailing you. The inclination toward disease can be passed on genetically, not only physiological diseases but also psychological, emotional, and spiritual ones.

Once again, just because a curse exists in your family line does not mean it has to land on you. You can always make healthy choices that will keep it at bay. If something has ever happened to ignite the curse, you may have gotten some inner healing for it. You may have sought out some deliverance or some prayer ministry, which stopped the curse from growing and being inflamed.

But the curse may linger there, just biding its time. The devil knows he has a long time. He's been waiting and working for thousands of years. He does know that his time is getting short now, so that may be why we're seeing the reactivation of so many ancient curses in this generation. Yet when godly intervention neutralizes a curse for a generation or a time, the devil just sits back and says, "Well, we'll see what will happen in the next generation." He is not locked into the same time/space continuum as we are. He does not think in terms of a basic human lifespan. He's not urgent about doing evil if he doesn't have the opportunity. His timeframe isn't 70 or 80 years, but rather 700 or 800 or whatever it takes. If he doesn't get anywhere in this generation, his demons aren't going anywhere. They do not die.

I am convinced that somewhere in hell there is a hit list, and this list catalogues all the curses. Satan looks at them and says, "Hmmmm…George is really a good guy. Eighty-seven generations ago he had a pervert in his blood line, but I can't get him to do that type of thing. Well, never mind. We'll just see what happens to George's kids or grandchildren. We have time."

THE SPECIFICITY OF CURSES

Curses cannot be broken decisively without exacting information, because the most effective way to break them is to reverse what happened in the first place. This applies both to curses that were invoked by ritualism and those that came from a specific behavior.

You need to find out as much as possible, asking who, how, what, when, where, and why:

1. *Who:* Who created the curse? Was it an ancestor or an unrelated person?

2. *How:* How was the curse created? Was it ceremonial (ritual) or genetic (ancestral). Was it by bloodline or by fiat (a declarative, commanding act of someone's will)?

3. *What:* What is the nature of the curse, for example does it relate to death, health, poverty, sex?

4. *When:* When was the curse initiated? Was it by a living person or someone who is no longer living? Was the person known to the victim or did it happen in ages past?

5. *Where:* What is the geographical location? Knowing this gives clues as to the root nature of the curse.

6. *Why:* What harm was intended by the curse? For example, to pass on an ungodly psychic gift, to victimize sexually, to create a death obsession?

A curse invoked by ritualism may only be broken by a reversal of the ritual in some manner. You do not always have to do it exactly the way it was done in the first place, but it can help to find out what happened. A case in point: I was working with a woman who had once written out blasphemies against God on a little scroll. To help reverse the curse, I had her perform the opposite. She wrote out blessings on another little scroll, and she kept it in her possession just as she had once done with the first scroll.

I have ministered to people who had participated in some very archaic, exotic rituals, and I have been able to find a counterpart for those rituals in Leviticus. This is because the most highly developed forms of black magic in secret societies almost always is based on spiritual law, and their rituals often involve a twisting or perversion of ancient ceremonies of Israel.

The same idea can help with curses that have resulted from a specific behavior. If someone was cursed by his father, then I bless him as a father, a Christian leader, and a pastor. This works particularly well if I am of the same gender as the person who originated the curse. When the Pope visited the United States and spoke to the victims of sexual abuse by priests, he helped to reverse the curse of abuse for those people. He acknowledged the guilt of the institution that had cursed them, speaking forgiveness and blessing them. When the Southern Baptists issued a formal apology for slavery, they helped to reverse the curse that was incurred at the time of the Civil War when they were adamantly pro-slavery. When the Canadian government issued an apology to First Nations people because of their past treatment of them, they helped loosen the hold of the curse that had been perpetrated when their predecessors in government took the people away from their homes and tried to force them to assimilate with the dominant North American culture, many times along with serious personal offenses.

Apologies, asking for forgiveness for specific injustices and injuries—these can prove to be very important for undoing the power of curses.

TURNING CURSES INTO BLESSINGS

Curse breaking is not as simple as saying, "Out, in the name of Jesus." Why does it have to be so complicated? After all, it doesn't seem to have been so difficult for Jesus and His first disciples. Consider the fact that time has piled up more obstacles. The devil has had over 2000 years since the time of Jesus to exercise his strategies, 2000 additional years to get his game plan going, to come up with more curses, to embed those curses, and to degenerate human civilization. We need more power than they had in the early Church because we need to do greater things than they did. In many ways, Peter, James, John, and Paul had it easy compared to us.

The Bible tells us that in the time to come there will be no more curses. In the throne room of God, the Lamb will reign supreme, and His people will serve Him with complete freedom. That is our hope.

If there is a time coming when all curses will be vanquished, and since we have not yet reached that time, then we need to commit ourselves to the task before us, which is to wrestle and labor with the help of the Holy Spirit against the multitude of curses that throng our existence.

We need to be intentional about turning curses into blessings, just as God does. I am convinced that people who have been targeted by curses are the same people who have the potential for great blessing. The devil, not wanting to waste his resources, goes after the people who have the greatest opportunity to do something great for God's Kingdom. He not only tries to stop them, but he also takes aim at their very destiny, at the center of their anointing.

Satan can see your anointing and your calling ahead of time. At your conception and birth, he can see where your blessings will fall, and he goes to work to undermine them. His plan is to turn your blessings into curses wherever possible.

One way you can help defeat him is to convert curses into blessings, purposefully, everywhere you go. I do it for other people all the time, and so can you. Wherever I go, I speak a pastoral blessing over the people of God. Every night when I'm not on the road, I speak a blessing over my children. Even when I am away from home, I do it by phone if at all possible. As we conclude the day, I have a prayer with each child individually, before my wife and I put each of them to bed. I use the same kinds of words over and over: "I speak to you health, prosperity, blessing, goodness, honor, and favor from God." I want the last thing our children hear as they drop off to sleep to be a word of blessing from their father.

Curse Breaking

Bless your own children. Bless your spouse. Bless the people around you. Bless your pastor. You never know who has a curse that needs to be broken. Live a lifestyle of blessing. By means of your words of blessing, invisible curses can be turned into tangible blessings.

Chapter 2

CURSES OF CONDUCT

In a public ministry session, I asked a woman named Marie to tell me a little bit about where her inner pain came from. "It was a whole bunch of stuff," she answered. "Being sexually abused as a child and having to hold it in for a very long time. No one would believe me."

I started to lead her in a curse-breaking prayer: "Everything my ancestors did…"

"Everything my ancestors did…"

"…to serve the devil…"

"…to serve the devil…"

"…I renounce…"

"…I renounce…"

"…in the name of Jesus Christ…"

(Silence.)

"Satan, get out of the way." I spoke forcefully to the demon that suddenly manifested with growling and violent writhing. One of my assistants took hold of the woman to keep her kicks from hitting me.

"Get out of the way. I am talking to Marie. Go. Satan, you took her when she was a child and brought abuse on her because of what her ancestors did. And then you tormented her when her family didn't believe her. Tell me your name."

Randy. (Sometimes, demons will assume the human name of the one who started the curse, such as "the curse of Randy.")

"Is that the name of the man who abused her?" All I got for an answer was a harsh shout.

"OK, Marie, let's take care of this. We must break the curse of the man who abused you and cast out the demon who has taken that name. Repeat after me: 'I, Marie...'"

"I, Marie..."

"...break the curse of Randy..."

"...break the curse of Randy..."

"The curse is broken...."

(Silence.) A new struggle ensued.

"Marie, say, 'the curse is broken.' Say it with me, 'the curse of Randy is broken.' Say it."

(With effort—) "...The curse...of Randy...is broken."

"Spirit of Abuse, get away from Marie. You do not have rights to her anymore." I called forth the demon to a state of manifestation, forcing him to lift the curse.

"Repeat after me. Say, 'I, Abuse...'"

I, Abuse...

"...lift the curse..."

...lift the curse...

"...on Marie, and on future generations..."

...on Marie, and on future generations...

"...and we all..."

...and we all...

"...go..."

...go...

"...now..."

...now...

"...to..."

...to...

"...the..."

...the...

"...pit!"

...pit!

The watching audience shouted for joy at such a dramatic display of God's power, and then everything got quiet. I spoke to Marie as she sat on the stage, somewhat overcome. "I want to ask you a question, Marie. Who did this for you?"

"Jesus."

"Who has the power?"

"Jesus does."

Marie went home a changed woman, no longer angry, defensive, or depressed as she had been before. I found out later that she was a professional kick boxer, which explained why she was solid muscle. No wonder I needed my assistant's help that day to keep her feet from taking me out! I have seen her since, and she is still walking in freedom from that awful, tormenting spirit of Abuse that had filled her with fear and bitterness.

ACTIONS BRING CURSES

The way family members and other people treat a child verbally and emotionally very much affects the child's development, for better or for worse. Children who are valued and protected from harmful influences have a much better chance of maturing into secure adults who can relate to others in a healthy way.

Children who suffer neglect or abuse, however, will require counseling, inner healing, and deliverance later in life. Almost always, ill treatment will bring spiritual devastation to a child's life. Being spoken to or treated in a negative, unloving way will typically result in what I call a "curse of conduct" on a child's life.

What Others Did or Didn't Say

Most of us are familiar with the effects of wounding words. "I hate you" cannot easily be erased from a child's vulnerable spirit.

But significant curses can also accompany what was not said. Parents who never utter the words "I love you" leave a child wondering. Maybe Mom and Dad love me, even though they never say it. But maybe they don't. Such children never know for sure, especially in times of difficulty. Every child needs individual, verbal affirmation.

All of us are emotional revisionists. We tend to rewrite our history, wishing things had been a certain way, not wanting to get stuck in the pain of the past. So we gloss over things like that. "Well, my parents were not very expressive people. They didn't know how important it was. I am sure they meant well. I love them, and we have a great relationship." This sidesteps the likelihood that their lack of verbal affirmation left a demonic opening at the time the emotional wounding took place and has resulted in a curse. It is not difficult to repair the breach and receive inner healing, but it can be difficult to accept the idea that help is needed.

"I love you"—if it is upheld by loving actions—is one of the best ways of saying "I value you." If your parents and others who should have valued your life never expressed their appreciation for your worth or their concern for your welfare, their failure to do so may have left you wondering if you are worth much. Value and worth can be expressed both in verbal and nonverbal ways, starting very young. In fact, if it has not been adequately expressed by the time a child is three years old, much damage has already been done. Your identity imprint was formed at that early stage of development, and it has been based upon what others did or didn't say to you about your value.

For the rest of your life, you may find that you are trying to earn approval—or running away from potential failure. Satan can use the silence to curse you with feelings of rejection even if you were not openly rejected. It may not seem too bad on the surface. They may not have told you explicitly, "I wish you hadn't been born," or "You have made my life miserable," but the absence of positive reinforcement may have left you wondering about your significance. The silence incurs a curse.

Small children need lots of hugs and kisses and affirmations. "Attaboys" and "attagirls" should be frequent to give a child an honest sense of his or her true significance.

What Others Did or Didn't Do

A child growing up in a non-affirmative environment may not realize at the time that anything is missing. To the child, it seems normal. Later in life, however, when it turns out to be difficult to affirm and love others, the grown child may realize the considerable influence, years earlier, of the conduct of parents and other adults. Such children—and you may be one of them—do not find it natural to show affection. Often they have "relationship issues." Instinctive warmth is absent or restrained.

What about commitments and remembrances that were ignored? The baseball game that Dad failed to come and watch, the birthday that was forgotten—these may be excused or forgotten by the child, but such instances leave a hole in the heart that the enemy may later try to fill with anger and bitterness. As children develop and as they commit themselves to a marriage partner, any kind of negligence regarding important milestones, as well as inattention to emotional hurts and struggles, can stir up a curse of resentment.

You can head off such an outcome with your own children regardless of their age. I can't express how healing it was to have my elderly parents start to say, "I love you, Bob" in a sincere effort to make up for their lack in the past. Not long ago, with my own middle child, I had a chance to practice what I preach. For five months I had been involved with a brutally intense shooting schedule for a reality TV show. I was completely mentally preoccupied five days a week, twelve hours a day. Then on the sixth day, I would fly somewhere to conduct a seminar, and on the seventh day fly back home to teach a local deliverance team. In the midst of that time came my daughter's birthday, and I wasn't going to be able to be present for the celebration. To rectify the situation, I promised her a trip with me when I went to conduct one of the seminars.

Well, it so happened that the shooting schedule got rearranged so I could be with her on her birthday. Now, you would think that having done that we could forget about the daddy trip, right? No, sir. "Dad, you said you were taking me to Seattle." So I made good on that promise. We went to the top of the Space Needle in the middle of a snowstorm when there was zero visibility, and we took a horseback ride in a snowstorm with rain and hail. But it didn't matter to her. She got her trip. And that's one less situation that the enemy could take advantage of.

Cursing Comments May Be Well Intentioned

Many times I have ministered to someone and discovered some deep, dramatic, demonic bondage that goes back to what might seem to have been a relatively insignificant event. Often it was some offhand comment, some caustic expression that at the time may have been intended to be humorous. The person may not have intended to be hurtful at all, but if the verbal slight gets backed up by inappropriate actions, the damage may be permanent.

Although no harm was intended, the end effect is to diminish the value of the other person. People brush it off: "There was no harm intended. I didn't think it would matter anyway." We assume how the other person would feel about a matter, making light of something that he or she considered truly important.

"You wouldn't have been interested." This assumption makes conclusions for people that they may not have made for themselves. It hijacks the decision making from them about something about which they might at least have wanted a chance to say no.

"I did what I thought was best for you." Yes, but where was the option to reconsider the issue? True statement as it may be, it may also be a way of arrogantly ignoring someone's needs. A shrug of the shoulders is not the same as an apology or an acknowledgment of the other person's perceptions.

Satan looks for these little things to pounce on. It doesn't take much for statements like these to open the door to an unintentional curse, particularly if an ancestral curse lies under the surface. Remember the words of the Bible: "Be sober, be vigilant; because your adversary the devil walks about like a roaring lion, seeking whom he may devour" (1 Pet. 5:8).

We need to be on the lookout for inappropriate statements and neglectful actions that can crack the door open for the enemy. We certainly do not need to become paranoid about such things, constantly worrying about every word we say. But we do carry a responsibility toward our family members and the people around us, lest their preexisting feelings of insignificance or rejection snowball into a bigger problem.

The Worst Curse of Conduct—Sexual Violation

In my estimation, sexual abuse may be the most evil of all the things that can happen to a person, especially when it happens to an innocent and helpless child. Sexual violation is the worst way to eradicate someone's integrity and self-worth because a person's sexuality is the most vulnerable core of identity. When sexual identity is not protected and honored, no part of the world can be safe anymore unless and until the love of God brings healing, freedom, and wholeness.

Much sexual abuse happens to small children, even to babies. I have ministered to some people who suffered tragic sexual trauma at the hands of an adult before they were old enough to have the cognitive ability to make sense out of it, let alone the language skills to express what they were feeling. The damage to a child's spirit and psyche is such that without a miracle from God and some very long-term therapy, they will never recover. For the rest of their lives, those who have been sexually abused (both male and female) will find their world a very unsafe place. They will develop all kinds of phobias and defense mechanisms and self-injurious behavior to try to deal with their emotional wounds.

Because it so thoroughly violates someone's physical, emotional, and spiritual wholeness, sexual exploitation invites a swarm of serious curses into that person's life.

Mentally Damaging Conduct

The curse of mentally damaging conduct has lasting effects that continue long after the person whose conduct initiated the curse has left. Mental damage becomes intertwined with spiritual damage to twist life into a maze with no escape—unless the curse can be broken and the sufferer can be nurtured back to wholeness.

Psychoses are often an escape from the memories of brutal mental mistreatment. The person's mind retreats from reality in an attempt to curtail the pain. Mental delusions provide a kind of relief.

Too often, people imitate what they have observed and even embrace what they hate. It seems irrational, but that is the nature of mental damage. In my experience of ministering inner healing to people who have mental health issues, people who are suffering from some kind of delusional disorder, up to the point of complete psychosis, have suffered some terribly damaging experience in the past, something so severe that their only means of survival to avoid suicide or total mental incapacitation is, at least from time to time and to varying degrees, to retreat into an alternate reality. Their minds cannot handle what happened. They are on overload, and they need a safety valve.

Repressed memories can be the most difficult sources of damage to deal with. Some unknown incident—unknown either because it happened when a person was very young or because the trauma drove the memory underground—acts like a toxin, poisoning body, mind, and emotions. Although the incident may seem to be absent from conscious memory, it dogs the person's life relentlessly.

Demons sometimes mask memories for the sake of perpetuating a curse in a person's life. Although it can seem cruel at the time of unmasking, I have found success in breaking such curses by commanding the demon to release the hidden memory. The upsurge of pain that accompanies the release seems to be almost too much to bear, but once the person is back in touch with the facts and feelings, healing and deliverance can follow swiftly. In the long run that may be the only pathway to breaking the curse that resulted from someone's conduct.

GETTING AT THE DEEP ROOTS

Curses of conduct can occur as a result of anyone's conduct, including your own. Whatever can wound the soul and spirit of a person can give entry to a curse.

Some inner scars are from self-inflicted wounds. The aftermath of a sinful action lingers in the form of the consequences to that action. You may sincerely regret your sinful action and repent of it, but in essence you have shot yourself in the foot. You can be forgiven for what you did, but it leaves a scar, and very often it affects subsequent circumstances of your life.

Let's say you got pregnant before you were married. One (most likely impulsive) moment of decision has had repercussions for you, for your child, for your partner, and for many others. You can't blame the devil for everything, but he has certainly been able to take advantage of what you did, to the point that you often can't sort out the good from the bad. Whether or not you added to your sin by getting an abortion, your life has been complicated. You suspect that some of your troubles fall into a curse-like pattern, but your efforts to tackle the symptoms have not started with the root, because you thought you dealt with that already.

Or let's say that you got raped. The deliberate conduct of someone else ruptured your life. Naturally that person was messed up or he would not have messed you up. It was an injury of intent. As time goes by, troubles pile up. You feel that you are laboring under an invisible cloud of a curse, and you want to cut it off so you can walk in freedom and grace. The words of the letter to the Hebrews have a personal application for you: "See to it that no one misses the grace of God and that no bitter root grows up to cause trouble and defile many" (Heb. 12:15 NIV). Only your Redeemer Jesus can heal and wipe out the inner damage and make it as if it were not, even as that decisive event must be retained as an actual part of your life history.

A third avenue for curses of conduct is what I call pain by proxy. Somebody else acted on your behalf, and you still feel the effects. A person who had the power to act on your behalf (kind of a spiritual power of attorney), such as a parent, a pastor, or a husband, made a curse-inducing declaration on your behalf.

This does not have to be a current event. It may not have been in your lifetime. Consider the transgenerational curses that I have alluded to already. To get at the deep root of a curse, you may need to go back many generations. You may be miserable today because somebody in your family line participated in some demonic ceremony or exercised some form of witchcraft. You may have been born with a wound, and no one knew about it. You just thought, That is just the way I am. Gotta live with it; this is how I have been hard-wired.

Yet you can't help it—you get agitated about your issues. You keep trying to get better. You would like to experience a degree of peace and joy. So far no amount of therapy or inner healing ministry has sufficed. The invisible wound festers, and you can almost see the enemy lurking nearby so he can probe it and irritate it.

It is time to get at the deep roots, time to dig them up for good, time to break the curse that came from ill-advised conduct. It is time to make sure it stays broken so that the healing can begin and so that the enemy no longer has anything he can take advantage of.

Chapter 3

THE CURSE OF ILLEGITIMACY

was in the midst of a teaching seminar when the Holy Spirit drew my attention to a sweet-looking young woman seated several rows from the front. Bible, cross, and anointing oil in hand, I slowly approached her. As I came within about 15 feet of where she was seated, the woman reacted violently. She stood to her feet, screaming and throwing chairs on either side of her. Those nearby fled in panic for safer sections of the hotel ballroom.

"Stay away from her, you can't have her," the demons inside the woman screamed. "She belongs to us. All the women in her bloodline belong to us."

With the help of several ministry assistants, I got her under control so that I could find out what demonic force had caused the outburst. We learned the woman's name was Cindy. Although she was Hispanic, the demon claimed to be a spirit of Death and Murder going back seven generations to a Chinese ancestor who tortured people before killing them. (It is not unusual to find odd ethnic ancestry quite unlike that of a cursed person. None of us has any idea to what parts of the world our ancestors may have traveled or with whom they may have consorted sexually, allowing unusual genetic concoctions in our bloodlines.)

As we explored Cindy's story further, we found that she had an illegitimate child through rape, she herself had been the product of rape, and her mother had been raped. I suspect that her grandmother, and so on, had likely suffered the same abuse, because that's how generational curses operate. Even though violence and the taking of human life had been the root of the curse, the demon bragged that it had been passed on, generation to generation, by sexual violence and the resulting illegitimacy. Cindy was eventually freed, but not without an intense struggle that required four large men to hold her frail body tightly to prevent me and others from being assaulted.

A Brief History of Illegitimacy

The curse of illegitimacy is one of the most frequent that I face in both public and private ministry, and I know that the reason it is one of the most prevalent curses of our time is because of the rampant immorality of our culture. Scripture and the law of the land have a lot to say about illegitimate birth, and spiritual reality reflects physical reality.

Legally speaking, the parents of illegitimate children were not married when the child was conceived. Spiritually speaking, people who carry a curse of illegitimacy have either inherited a pall of illegitimacy from ancestors who were born out of wedlock, or they themselves were conceived outside of marriage. Those who carry the burden of illegitimacy feel disqualified and disinherited, not only in their families of origin but also in the Kingdom of God. The curse of illegitimacy is a very common one, even in a society that has de-stigmatized the terminology.

In the past, only legitimate children could inherit the estates of their fathers. In the United States, a series of Supreme Court decisions in the 1970s abolished most of the legal consequences of bastardy (an almost-obsolete term), defining them as violations of the equal protection clause of the fourteenth amendment to the US Constitution. Before the turn of the twenty-first century, each of the 50 states had revised its legal code to give children born out of wedlock as well as adopted children the same rights to inherit their parents' property as children born to married parents.

Today in the Western world, many people do not know what illegitimacy is. If you use the word illegitimacy with many teenagers, you will get a blank stare. They find it difficult to pronounce the word. This is in spite of the fact that illegitimacy has grown to epidemic proportions, even in cultural enclaves traditionally considered immune to the problem.

In the 1950s, five percent of children born in the United States were born to unmarried mothers. By 2009, that figure had risen to 41 percent, an average that includes 73 percent of black children, 53 percent of Hispanic children, and 29 percent of white children.[1] As shocking as those numbers are, they are probably low because of underreporting. Enough stigma remains that people do not always report a birth as illegitimate. And those are not even the most recent statistics.

A BRIEF SCRIPTURAL HISTORY OF THE CURSE OF ILLEGITIMACY

Although in civil terms, illegitimacy has been legally destigmatized, the same is not true spiritually. A curse comes with it. You could even say that one of the reasons we have so many problems in this country is because we have unleashed the curse of illegitimacy upon ourselves.

Technically, the term means born of parents who are not married to each other, but in the spiritual sense, the curse of illegitimacy falls at the time of conception, and even if the parents "make it right" by getting married, their child can retain the effects of illegitimacy. In other words, the parents' decision to get married does not break the curse. Add to that the powerful currents of familial history and sinful conduct, and the number of people who struggle against an invisible curse of illegitimacy grows even larger. Illegitimate children are the product of rape, incest, fornication, or adultery.

Scripture gives reference to issues concerning illegitimate birth. For example:

> *When they go with their flocks and herds to seek the Lord, they will not find him; he has withdrawn himself from them. They are unfaithful to the Lord; they give birth to illegitimate children...* (Hosea 5:6-7 NIV).

> *...They said to Him, We are not illegitimate children and born out of fornication; we have one Father, even God* (John 8:41 AMP).

One of illegitimate birth shall not enter the assembly of the Lord; even to the tenth generation none of his descendants shall enter the assembly of the Lord (Deuteronomy 23:2).

As stated in the Book of Deuteronomy, the law of God for the Israelites stated that a person of illegitimate birth (which included the offspring of other forbidden marriages) was disallowed from the assembly of the Lord. Why to the tenth generation? Just as with the expression, to the third and fourth generation, which I mentioned in the first chapter, the number of generations is not meant to be taken literally. The expression is an idiom, and it means to convey a sense of the perpetuity of the curse. (In the Hebrew number system, the number ten is considered the number of perfection and completeness. Thus it indicates perpetuity.) So when the Law says that a curse will apply for ten generations, it does not imply that by the eleventh generation the curse will be over. It means that the restriction will continue forever.

Under Old Testament Law, someone who was designated a bastard could never join the congregation in worship. That was it. They had to stay on the outside. This produced very serious Old Covenant implications but also some significant New Covenant ramifications. Under the New Covenant, established when Jesus Christ came to fulfill the Law (see Romans 10:4), such a law no longer applies. But we need to distinguish the unseen results of the curse from the application of the Law. Believers are under God's grace, and they may be fully accepted into the congregation of the Lord. Any and all of us may come to church. We have been forgiven for our own sins and for the sins of our parents and ancestors. However, we may bring with us some of the consequences of the curse of illegitimacy, and it is important to understand how to activate our freedom in that regard.

Now it is true that remnants of the Old Covenant law remain in canon (Church) law:

Persons of illegitimate birth are forbidden by the canon law from receiving any of the minor orders without a dispensation from the bishop; nor can they in the Latin church be admitted to holy orders [i.e., the ministry] or to benefices with cure of souls [ecclesiastical offices accompanied by revenue or property such as a rectory or vicarage], except by a dispensation from the pope. In the Church of England a bastard cannot be admitted to orders without a dispensation from the sovereign or archbishop.[2]

The ancient Jews and the early Church fathers viewed human beings against the high order of the nature of God's creation, and they took very seriously anything that caused that to fall into disrepute. Adultery, rape, incest, fornication, as well as physical mutilation (whether intentional or unintentional) were seen as an affront to the divine order of creation.

Among the ancient Jews, persons of illegitimate birth could not claim paternal inheritance, nor could they even claim proper treatment as children in the family. This is what Hebrews 12:8 refers to when it draws the following contrast between the treatment that God's true children can expect and that given to people who are not related to Him as children:

> *And you have forgotten the exhortation which speaks to you as to sons: "My son, do not despise the chastening of the Lord, nor be discouraged when you are rebuked by Him; for whom the Lord loves He chastens, and scourges every son whom He receives." If you endure chastening, God deals with you as with sons; for what son is there whom a father does not chasten? But if you are without chastening, of which all have become partakers, then you are illegitimate and not sons* (Hebrews 12:5-8).

If all of this seems like too much nitpicking about legalities, just remember that the devil is the one who takes advantage of spiritual technicalities. He is always looking for the legal loopholes. That's the main reason we need to be crossing our spiritual t's and dotting our i's and wrapping up every aspect of a situation to the best of our ability.

SUMMARY OF FACTS ABOUT THE CURSE OF ILLEGITIMACY

The reason I have devoted an entire chapter to the curse of illegitimacy is because it is so prevalent in our culture. People who minister the freedom of deliverance to others run into it almost every time they minister.

Curse Breaking

Think about it. If the curse of illegitimacy remains in effect for more than ten generations, how could any of us escape? Each of us was born from the union of two people. Each of those people came from the union of two more, or four altogether. If you take it back eight generations, approximately to the time of Abraham Lincoln, each of us has 250 people who contributed to our genetic and spiritual heritage. If we keep going, the number rises exponentially. By the time we get back to the time of Shakespeare, we will have gotten up to 16,384 ancestors, and counting. Somewhere in that vast number of people will certainly be somebody who produced an illegitimate child. We are each the product of much good but also of an awful lot of evil. Much sin has gone by and many curses. Part of the problem is solved when we get saved, but not all of it gets solved. Not all of the curses are active in any one individual, but if we suspect the prior existence of any curse, we should break it.

Although you yourself may or may not have been conceived or born illegitimately, most if not all of us have come to faith carrying the curse of illegitimacy. After thousands of years of human history, how could anybody's bloodline not be tainted by illegitimate birth? Family lines are perpetuated by sexual activity, and sexual activity is rife with illicit acts, many of which result in pregnancy and the birth of babies. The curse may have been weakened over time (or reinforced, especially if you or your parents were born out of wedlock), but I believe that all of us need to deal with this curse sooner or later.

Here are four facts about the curse of illegitimacy that are essential for you to know. I will elaborate about each one below:

1. This curse falls on progeny of adultery, rape, incest, and fornication.

2. This curse lasts forever.

3. This curse cannot be broken by legitimizing a marriage.

4. The grace of God in the New Covenant supersedes the Old Covenant.

1.   This curse falls on progeny of adultery, rape, incest, and fornication. This includes any unsanctioned encounter (unsanctioned biblically or morally) that results in childbirth. This may also include some forms of surrogacy. (Look at the problems Abraham and his descendants have had with Ishmael.) The ability of the devil to torment the child—and the parents as well—with the curse of illegitimacy relates to the state in which a man and a woman found themselves when they came together in sexual union outside of biblical, lawful marriage

2.   This curse lasts forever. As stated earlier, the number ten indicated completeness to the Hebrew people. In breaking the curse of illegitimacy, not only are we dealing with a basic principle ("a curse isn't broken until it's broken"), but we are dealing with a specific biblical edict that declares in black and white: "this curse lasts forever"—that is, until it gets broken by the power of God once and for all.

3.   This curse cannot be broken by legitimizing a marriage. In terms of the curse, it does not matter if the parents eventually marry. From the perspective of civil or canon law, marriage does legitimize the birth, and of course the child will more likely have a stable environment if the parents marry.

4.   The grace of God in the New Covenant supersedes the Old Covenant. The "forever" of the Old Covenant becomes the "never" of the New Covenant, by the blood of Jesus Christ. This is vital to understand, especially if you yourself are the product of illegitimate conception and birth. I have no intention of putting you on a guilt trip. Complete freedom from the curse is within your reach, and you should be fully able to enter into the life of the Church in any way that your calling takes you, with nothing holding you back.

HOW TO IDENTIFY THE CURSE OF ILLEGITIMACY

How can you tell if the difficulties you or another person experience might be coming from a curse of illegitimacy? I see four reliable indicators, as follows: (1) Trouble in worship, prayer, and giving; (2) Trouble reading the Bible; (3) Discomfort in fellowship with believers; and (4) Constant questioning of one's salvation.

In other words, you will find an inherent, instinctive opposition to life in the Church. People who have a curse of illegitimacy will find attending church to be a challenge. They may tend to be loners and to be sporadic in their church attendance. They may not enjoy corporate worship or being around other members of the Body of Christ. They will not be faithful in giving their tithes and offerings because the curse constantly impedes them.

Even reading the Bible alone can be difficult. Not only do they lack the desire to read the Word, but they often find it difficult to comprehend. People who suffer from this curse have told me, "I try to read the Bible. I just don't get it. Truthfully, I rarely have a desire to read it."

Just as with corporate worship, any fellowship gathering makes these people uncomfortable. They find it unnatural to be drawn to relationships with people of faith. People with the curse of illegitimacy do not like to hang out with others in the Body of Christ. They do not like church social activities in the first place, but if they do come to a church service or a church event, they will be the ones who slip out the door the minute it's over.

It is not because someone has lectured them, saying, "You don't belong here. You shouldn't come to church." Nobody needs to say anything, because these people possess an instinctive response to gatherings of fellow Christians: I am not welcome. I don't feel comfortable. They do not process this information cognitively. They have not researched the Levitical proscriptions or compared themselves to outcasts. They just feel it deep inside, and the demons attached to this curse cause these people to feel unsafe.

Sometimes these are the people who come forward repeatedly for altar calls, unsure of their salvation. They return again and again for prayer ministry, seeking help with their insecurities about how they feel in terms of their fellowship with God, the house of God, and the people of God. They never feel released into their spiritual gifts, and they are never sure about their spiritual destiny.

Such insecurity is one of the effects of the curse of illegitimacy. They are not comfortable in church, and they cannot connect with other church people no matter what they do. They do show up, and they go through the motions, because they know they need to. They hunger to worship God and to be in His presence. But they never quite feel comfortable.

Lost to their view is the fact that Old Covenant injunctions are hanging over their heads. The curse is operating the way it was set up to do, and it is holding them back from appropriating the New Covenant grace and mercy of the blood of Christ. They are still stuck, and they do not know what to do.

BREAKING THE CURSE OF ILLEGITIMACY

So what can you do about the curse of illegitimacy?

First of all, if your ancestors committed acts that led to illegitimacy and one or more of your ancestors were born illegitimately, then you have a right to renounce the curses that their acts brought about. If you have a child who is not yet of legal age (18 years old), you can break the curse on behalf of the child, because you are the voice of authority for the bloodline of the child.

If the father is available and willing, he should break the curse on behalf of his child. If the father or husband refuses to take spiritual responsibility for the child, the mother can break the curse. This applies frequently because of absent fathers, divorce, and marital separation. The mother can declare that she is the Bride of Christ and that the authority of the Lord replaces that of the father as head of the home.

The curse of illegitimacy is what I call a core curse. It proves to be foundational to much of what the devil does in people's lives. I would consider some other curses to be tangential. Satan can use them or not. But core curses are fundamental to civilization, central to human relationships. Satan knows how to build on them. Therefore, it is up to us to know how to get rid of them.

I have seen some incredible relief when this curse gets broken. It is almost instantaneous. And it can happen for you right now. If you are the offspring of illegitimacy, or if you are the parent of an illegitimate child, please take a moment to repeat this prayer:

A Prayer of Renunciation to Break the Curse of Illegitimacy

I, _____, confess the Lord Jesus Christ as my Savior, and I renounce the kingdom of darkness, along with all the works of the devil. I renounce all sins of my ancestors back to Adam and Eve and everyone in between. I especially renounce all sexual sins of my ancestors and in particular the sins of adultery, fornication, rape, and incest. If any of my ancestors committed these sins, I declare their effect on me to be null and void. If I am the parent of any illegitimate child and that child is not of legal consent in his or her country of domicile, I speak for that child, and I declare that the curse of illegitimacy upon him or her is broken by virtue of the power of the blood of Christ and the authority I have in His name. This curse of illegitimacy is now broken and renounced to the tenth generation and into perpetuity. This declaration is binding upon all demonic forces that have hitherto exercised any influence because of this curse. Every effect of this curse is broken, including all hindrances to worship, prayer, giving, acts of charity, reading of God's Word, attendance at the house of God, and any inhibitions regarding Christian fellowship and Christian communion. I declare that all of this is legal and binding on earth and in Heaven. I and any illegitimate offspring of mine are free from this curse and henceforth have every right to enter fully into personal relationship with God, enjoying the full benefits of corporate worship, including receiving the body and blood of our Lord Jesus Christ through communion. In the name of the Father, the Son, and the Holy Spirit, the curse of illegitimacy is broken! Amen.

ENDNOTES

1. *National Vital Statistics Reports* 59, no. 3 (December 21, 2010), accessed August 20, 2012, www.cdc.gov/nchs/data/nvsr/nvsr59/nvsr59_03.pdf?loc=interstitialskip. See also "Our view on kids: When unwed births hit 41%, it's just not right," *USA Today* (January 25, 2011).

2. *The New Unger's Bible Dictionary*, Merrill Unger, R.K. Harrison, eds. (Chicago: Moody, 2006), s.v. "Bastard."

Chapter 4

WORD CURSES

I ministered to a young man whose father was a pastor. Anyone who would have met this teenager in a youth group would have thought he was the coolest Christian kid on the block. But he was a very troubled boy, and part of him was so angry with his father that he wanted to kill him.

This aggressive anger, so severe he wanted to see his father dead, was not just part of a passing adolescent flare-up. It had roots in a specific incident that had happened a few years before. Wounding words had been spoken to him by his father, and the grave consequences (unknown to the father) included demonic involvement and the boy's meticulous plotting to make sure that his father would die for speaking such words to him.

His father's church was a small one, and apparently he had not been able to achieve much visible success in life. My guess is that the father probably carried a lot of issues related to how he felt about himself and his life. He was depressed and grumpy much of the time.

When the boy was younger, he was driven by ambition. One day, he looked up at his dad with a big grin on his face and said, "You know what, Daddy? When I grow up I am going to go to Harvard, and I'm going to be a doctor someday."

What did his father say? Did he encourage what might seem to him to be a pipe dream? Did he pat his son on the head and deliver a bland affirmation? No, the man looked at his son and said, "Shut up. I do not want to hear that kind of talk in this house. Nobody in this house is going to Harvard, and nobody in this house is ever going to become a doctor, and that's that. Nobody is going to amount to anything. Stop this foolishness. Drop it. Do not ever bring it up again."

The boy was devastated. He had been genuinely excited about the prospect of becoming a Harvard-trained doctor. He knew his father's reaction was way out of proportion to what he had said, but the words had already done their damage. His heart began to curl and dry up.

Now anyone can understand that he had probably caught his father at an especially bad moment. Never mind that it is good for children to dream dreams and to have noble desires. Some people might even excuse him by saying, "Well, he did not want his child to have unreasonable expectations and then to have his hopes dashed later because the family was never going to be in a position to provide those kinds of opportunities."

But the Bible says, "Fathers, do not provoke your children to wrath…" (Eph. 6:4), and that single provocation provided a big enough opening for a demon and a curse.

The boy never mentioned it again to his father, but he could not stop thinking about the words his father had spoken. He began to flounder in school (whereas before he had been an excellent student, quite possibly Harvard material). And he began to fantasize about how he might actually murder his own father.

Of course, the father knew nothing about this. Eventually, the young man became alarmed at his increasingly erratic behavior and his deeply-seated hatred toward his father. He came to one of our seminars seeking help. As he shared his story with me, I recognized that the persistent animosity he held toward his farther had become on opening for serious demonic oppression. This led to an exorcism of a spirit of Murder that had entered because the word curse spoken by his father had led to sustained bitterness. Once the curse was broken and the demon of Murder was expelled, the young man began the process of reconstructing his life and his dream.

UNDERSTANDING WORDS THAT WOUND

The human tongue is a powerful force. Every one of us knows this from personal experience. Remember what James wrote to the early Christians:

> *For we all stumble in many things. If anyone does not stumble in word, he is a perfect man, able also to bridle the whole body. Indeed, we put bits in horses' mouths that they may obey us, and we turn their whole body. Look also at ships: although they are so large and are driven by fierce winds, they are turned by a very small rudder wherever the pilot desires. Even so the tongue is a little member and boasts great things.*
>
> *See how great a forest a little fire kindles! And the tongue is a fire, a world of iniquity. The tongue is so set among our members that it defiles the whole body, and sets on fire the course of nature; and it is set on fire by hell. For every kind of beast and bird, of reptile and creature of the sea, is tamed and has been tamed by mankind. But no man can tame the tongue. It is an unruly evil, full of deadly poison. With it we bless our God and Father, and with it we curse men, who have been made in the similitude of God. Out of the same mouth proceed blessing and cursing. My brethren, these things ought not to be so* (James 3:2-10).

Every person on earth has been affected by the power of the tongue, both positively and negatively. When words carry poison, the results are like forest fires and ocean tempests, and other people get caught up in the fallout, sometimes to their grave detriment. The enemy watches for opportunities to inflict his torture on the people who have been wounded by the words of others, people whose tormented hearts lie wide open to his demonic infestation. All varieties of curses can be activated by as little as a single evil word, especially when uttered by someone who carries authority over the one spoken to, such as when a father or mother speaks to one of their children.

Along with the communication of wicked words come curses as reliably as "A" follows "B," because that is the way God set it up. Therefore, we should be diligent to avoid words that bring darkness, both in speaking them out and (insofar as it depends upon us) receiving such curse-inducing words from others. Our assignment is to bring light into the darkest situations.

Paul's divinely inspired advice applies not only to the people to whom he wrote his epistles, but also to us today:

> *Let no one deceive you with empty words, for because of such things God's wrath comes on those who are disobedient. Therefore do not be partners with them.*
>
> *For you were once darkness, but now you are light in the Lord. Live as children of light* (for the fruit of the light consists in all goodness, righteousness and truth) *and find out what pleases the Lord. Have nothing to do with the fruitless deeds of darkness, but rather expose them* (Ephesians 5:6-11 NIV).

EXPOSING WORDS OF DARKNESS

What are empty words ("vain words" in the King James Version)? Not only are they words of spiritual deception within the realm of theology that are intended to deceive people, but they include any words spoken without regard to their hurtful effect on others. They are words that wound. The resulting wounds may never heal in a person's lifetime. In fact, often they engender curses that carry on down through the family line from that time forward.

Sometimes we think that negative actions outstrip mere words in their damaging effects, but too often what comes out of a person's mouth is much more caustic, longer-lasting, and more penetrating than the actions by themselves.

Beware of your own words. Jesus warned us that for every idle (empty, vain) word that we speak, we will be held accountable on the Day of Judgment:

A good man out of the good treasure of his heart brings forth good things, and an evil man out of the evil treasure brings forth evil things. But I say to you that for every idle word men may speak, they will give account of it in the day of judgment. For by your words you will be justified, and by your words you will be condemned (Matthew 12:35-37).

Idle words will be taken at face value by the devil. It does not matter if you did not really mean what you said. He will seize on the words and run with them, causing trouble for the person spoken to as well as for the speaker, doing as much damage as he possibly can get away with.

When the father in the story above told his son that he and nobody else in that family would ever amount to anything, that was a statement of fact as far as the devil was concerned. He skewered the boy's heart with that statement, and the poison began to have its effect. The trajectory of the curse was set. Because the father never retracted his own statement or broke the curse he had engendered, it was as if the boy was caught in a spider web. His only hope of escape lay in the future, when with God's help he could break the curse and step free.

EXAMPLES OF WORDS THAT WOUND

Almost nobody means it when they voice words that wound. But the curse-inducing effect is the same as if they did. Satan pounces on words that wound and he carries them out to the limits of their literal meaning. Remember that the next time you hear (or are tempted to say) a statement such as "Go to hell!" or "Goddamn you!" or "I'll be goddamned." The ultimate meaning may not be realized instantaneously, of course. But a death wish may well be followed by a lifetime of misery. One day, time will run out.

When a person tells someone to "F——— off," what is that person really saying? Is it just a commonplace expression in our culture today, just a hip way of saying, "Don't bug me. Get off my case"? Sadly, it is more than that. When we use profane or damning words in any kind of conversational exchange, we bring a curse on the person spoken to—and the curse comes back on us into the bargain. In this case, we desacralize the deepest significance of our spirituality. We make emotional and physical intimacy a crude four-letter word, rather than an expression of profound, personal self-expression. Sex is reduced to an epithet, divorcing it from the context of caring communication.

Sometimes our statements are against ourselves, and such vows, spoken in moments of passion and frustration, bring an additional curse on our own heads. We reap what we sow. (See Job 4:8; Proverbs 22:8; Hosea 10:13; Galatians 6:7-8.) When evil words are sown, a harvest of curses and pain is guaranteed.

A wife says to her husband, "I wish you were dead."

Depressed beyond caring, a girl sighs, "I wish I were dead."

In a moment of exasperation, a mother tells her daughter, "I wish you'd never been born."

Later, the daughter compounds the curse by saying, "I wish I had never been born."

A husband looks down at his wife and spits out, "I just wish I hadn't married you."

Another husband, who is also a father, finds opportunities to make derogatory comments to his son. Finally one day he caps them off with: "My life was great until you came along."

How often have we heard (or declared), "I'll never speak with him again." "I will never do _____ again!" "I never want to see him again." Such words beget a curse. Speakers of such words are binding themselves with a vow. They are committing themselves to a course of action that is disobedient to what Christ has taught.

We do not realize what we're doing when we make a vow. A vow is a solemn declaration of evil by written or spoken intent. I could take you on a whole biblical journey to explore the horrible things that have happened as a result of vows that people made. For example, do you remember what happened to Jephthah's daughter? You can read the story in Judges 11. Jephthah was the son of a man named Gilead and a harlot. His half-brothers drove him out of the family. As an adult, he led the Israelites into a war with the Ammonites. Military success was within his reach, but just to make sure he would win the battle, he made a vow to the Lord. He vowed to sacrifice whatever would first come out of his house to meet him when he returned home, probably assuming that it would be some animal that would be acceptable for a burnt sacrifice. After his victory over the Ammonites, he returned to his home. Who should come out the door to greet him but his beloved only daughter? Jephthah was devastated at what he had done, but he was bound by his vow to carry it out. After giving the girl two months' time to mourn with her friends, he killed his own daughter. (Some commentators think he may not have actually slain her, but instead consigned her to perpetual virginity, a condition that was akin to a death sentence in ancient Israel. Either way, it was a horrible end to his hasty vow.)

Because vows are so serious, even Jesus warned in the New Testament: "Let your 'Yes' be 'Yes,' and your 'No,' 'No.' For whatever is more than these is from the evil one" (Matt. 5:37).

Then there are oaths, which serve as the authentication of vows. My definition of an oath is as follows: "the authentication of an evil purpose by affirming commitment to fulfillment."

What does an oath sound like? Commonly, we hear people say, "Well, I be damned if I will let _____ happen." Do they really want to be damned? Do they really know what they are saying? Do they really want to suffer eternal punishment in the fires of hell, separated from God? That is quite literally what they are calling down on their own heads when they affirm such a thing.

WHO SPEAKS WORDS THAT WOUND?

Besides speaking harmful words over our own lives, who else is guilty of speaking words that wound? Sworn enemies? Relative strangers who wish us ill because of something we have done to irritate them?

In actual fact, the people who speak the most wounding words to us will be the ones with whom we deal the most, our friends and family members. If you are old enough, you may remember a song by this name: "You Always Hurt the One You Love, the One You Shouldn't Hurt at All." There is a lot of truth in that.

We say terrible things to the people who are nearest to us. We would never say such things to a stranger. We think less about being cautious with our tongue when it comes to people with whom we are in a relationship.

Your foes may have slandered you and said hurtful things and that anonymous driver on the highway may have cussed you out, but none of that affects you much as something your spouse or your parents said. That is what cuts you to the quick. When people who should love you and care about you and protect you speak evil into your life, their words do considerable damage.

Parents automatically have spiritual authority over their children. If they abuse that authority, it is as if they just handed their children over into the hands of the enemy. A curse follows automatically, because someone in authority has decreed something harmful. It is worse if actions accompany the words. If a parent engages in incest with a child, that act gives legal permission for a demon to possess the child. If a parent verbally and emotionally abuses a child, demons will have been issued a carte blanche to attack that defenseless child, and they will not hesitate to do so.

When a parent shouts, "I wish you had never been born!" that gives the devil the right to put a curse of abandonment and a curse of rejection on the child. As I have ministered to people, I have had more than one tell me that their parents have said to them, "Well, I should have aborted you in the first place." Abortion is murder. These parents were willing to commit murder to get rid of their own child. And now those same children can't understand where their spirit of murder came from.

People have told me that when they were growing up, they were sick all the time and accidents seemed to happen to them more than to other people. Then after a while, it comes out that their parents told them something like, "I wish you would have died back then. I wish you hadn't survived. I wish you were dead because you make my life miserable." What a horrendous thing to say, and what a terrible, curse-filled burden to put on your own child.

A correlation to this happens sometimes when parents divorce. It is bad enough that children often blame themselves for their parents' marital problems and failure, but some parents go so far as to lay the whole blame directly at the child's feet, saying something like, "You know, we'd still be married if it weren't for you." How horrible is that? It is even more inexcusable when the father or stepfather sexually abused the child, and now not only is the mother steadfastly denying the sexual abuse, but now she's blaming a child for her marital breakup. She herself takes no responsibility for her lousy choice in men, and she makes a bad situation much worse by lashing out at her child.

Such parents are more common than you may think.

POISON PASTORS

After parents, pastors can be the next-worst offenders. Some pastors stand behind their pulpits and browbeat their congregations, causing untold grief to the men and women who are under their care. Have you ever heard a pastor get up and say something like, "I am going to tell what will happen to you if you ever leave this church"? If you have, that pastor essentially cursed you. Any pastor who has beaten up on the sheep like that is not someone you want to hang around. Such pastors must have their own demons to deal with, and they need help to get delivered.

So often when something like this happens, it is because pastors are shaking in their boots. They may feel that their control over their congregations is slipping, and they may be trying to compensate. Under the threat of losing reputation and livelihood, pastors can degenerate into speaking such evil. Pastors should be speaking hope and health and encouragement and blessing to the members of their flock, not browbeating them.

These pastors may not appear to be evil. They may not be loud. In fact, they may employ one of the best lead-ins in the book: "Now, I say this in love...." If they have to tell you they are saying it in love, you can already assume that it is not true. Brace yourself, because they are about to stick in the knife. Better still, slip out of that church fast.

It is more than OK to get out of a church if the pastor starts verbally beating up the congregation. It is far better to flee than to get dragged down farther by his words. I do not care if your grandma purchased the second pew on the left-hand side and there's a little plaque on there with your name on it. Let somebody else have it. I do not care how much money you've poured into that church and how much you hate to leave your investment behind; you had better just scurry out the back door as fast as you can!

While I am on the subject, let me also address another pastor-related problem. People come to me for ministry sometimes from churches whose pastors thunder from the pulpit that Christians cannot have demons. They come to us because they know many of their problems can be traced to demonic interference, and yet their pastor keeps putting people on a guilt trip by telling them to pray more, read the Bible more, give more, and do more for God, because that will solve every problem. The people may have gotten onto that treadmill for a while, but their problems only got worse.

Satan loves to interfere in a church that does not believe that he is real. In fact, pastors who make such a point of preaching that way essentially open the front door of the building to welcome in all sorts of demonic visitors. They supply an open invitation by ignoring and deliberately refuting the spiritual reality that Christians—including pastors—can be oppressed and tormented by demons as much as any unredeemed sinner.

If this is happening in your church, go someplace else. Find a church where you will get the whole truth.

SET YOUR MIND ON HIGHER THINGS

My aim has been to open your eyes to what may be going on around you. Words have power. When words of evil intent have been directed at you, you have suffered wounds. Those wounds may have become infected with curses and demons. Through your own efforts, you can counteract the effect of those words only to a degree. Sooner or later you must confront the curses, preferably in the company of a fellow Christian who can also speak words of healing and restoration to your mind and spirit.

As you move into wholeness, the words of the Bible provide the best advice of all:

> *If then you have been raised with Christ [to a new life, thus sharing His resurrection from the dead], aim at and seek the*

[rich, eternal treasures] that are above, where Christ is, seated at the right hand of God. And set your minds and keep them set on what is above (the higher things), *not on the things that are on the earth. For [as far as this world is concerned] you have died, and your [new, real] life is hidden with Christ in God....*

But now put away and rid yourselves [completely] of all these things: anger, rage, bad feeling toward others, curses and slander, and foulmouthed abuse and shameful utterances from your lips! Do not lie to one another, for you have stripped off the old (unregenerate) *self with its evil practices, and have clothed yourselves with the new [spiritual self], which is [ever in the process of being] renewed and remolded into [fuller and more perfect knowledge upon] knowledge after the image* (the likeness) *of Him Who created it* (Colossians 3:1-3, 8-10 AMP).

As you bring down word-engendered curses and resist the demons that have come with them, remember that Jesus Christ Himself is the living Word and most powerful word of all:

...His name is called The Word of God.... And He has on His robe and on His thigh a name written: King of kings and Lord of lords (Revelation 19:13, 16).

Let Him set you free!

Chapter 5

CURSES OF CULTS AND THE OCCULT

Sandra stood, asking for prayer, in one of our seminars. "I am tormented day and night," she said in anguished tones. "The demons never leave me alone. They move inside my body as if my flesh was crawling. Sometimes they lodge in my back or my spine. My whole body twitches at times like an electric current is surging through it." She wept uncontrollably and then whispered, "I am so ashamed. At times they come to me sexually and threaten to molest me."

I placed an arm around her shoulder as she dissolved into inconsolable crying. "Please help," she pleaded. "Someone told me that you understand these things and could help pray this evil away from me."

"Are you a Christian?"

"Yes," she responded, then paused. "Well, not your kind of Christian."

"What does that mean?"

"I'm a Mormon."

My heart was touched by her obvious suffering and mental torment. But I knew that if she were to be free and break whatever curses had bound her, she needed complete spiritual transformation. "Your Jesus is not the Christian Jesus," I said. "The Mormon Jesus was supposedly born of a sexual relationship between God and Mary. And your Jesus was not always God. Joseph Smith Jr. taught that Jesus was once a human being like you and me, and he became a god."

Sandra stopping crying and grew tense. I could see her despair fading away and being replaced by hardness.

"I am sure you've heard it said in the Mormon Church, 'As man is now, God once was; as God is now, man may become.'"

Sandra nodded her head in acknowledgement.

"You can't believe that and be truly set free," I admonished her. "I'll be happy to show you how to break these curses, but you must first understand it isn't me who breaks the curses; it is the power of Jesus. And you must put your faith in the right Jesus, the one who is God now and has always been God from eternity past. All I ask you to do is place your trust in Christ as being fully God, uncreated and eternal, and renounce Joseph Smith Jr. as a false prophet."

"No! Never!" Sandra screamed, as she turned and ran from the meeting room, never to be seen again.

Of course, I could have humored her and accommodated her differing religious persuasion, but commiserating with her condition was not what she needed. Spiritual freedom for Sandra required putting her full faith in Jesus Christ as God in order for all her curses to be broken and her torment lifted. It would have been disingenuous and unbiblical of me to suggest otherwise.

WHAT IS A CULT?

Before I get into the details about identifying and breaking the kinds of curses that come along with cults, I need to give you a basic definition of cult. I am referring specifically to religious cults, groups that cultivate devotion to deities and spirits other than the three-in-one Father, Son, and Holy Spirit.

For an encyclopedic approach to understanding cults, please refer to my book, *Larson's Book of World Religions and Alternative Spirituality*, which has become a respected reference volume in Christian circles. In addition to almost 600 pages of text, that book contains a long resource list for further reading.

In the introductory pages of that book, I define the key characteristics of a cult:

Many of the groups identified as cults share the following common characteristics:

1. A centralized authority that tightly structures both philosophy and lifestyle

2. An "us versus them" complex, pitting the supposedly superior insights of the group against a hostile outside culture

3. A commitment for each member to proselytize intensively the unconverted

4. An entrenched isolationism that divorces the devotee from the realities of the world at large[1]

Let me add the following, also from that same book:

[Cult] membership is divided between established groups with reasonably respectable followings (such as Mormonism, Christian Science, Unity) and less institutional movements (New Age). But fundamentally, all non-Christian groups have one thing in common: They consider the claims of Christ to be optional, not essential to salvation.[2]

In this book you are reading, for the most part I will stick with describing the specifically non-Christian groups that Christians most widely acknowledge as cults. I will not be making the finer distinctions between divergent points of view among believers, who sometimes hold that other Christian groups have become cults. If I seem to hold up as examples the same few cults repeatedly, it will only be because most people recognize them as such, not because the same information does not apply to many other groupings of people.

Most of my readers will be from the English-speaking Western world, so I will not detail the bewildering array of cults that can be found elsewhere in the world, except as some of them have been imported to pockets of our society. In any case, this chapter and the next one are not meant to focus as much on details of false belief systems as they are on the curse factor.

The next chapter, "Curses of Clandestine Cults," will focus on curses associated with cults that keep many of their ritualistic practices shrouded in secrecy for all but committed members. In this chapter, I will endeavor to describe cults and their accompanying curses in more general terms.

BONDAGE TO A BELIEF SYSTEM

A curse of cults results from a belief system that controls the thinking of people to the extent that their view of spiritual reality becomes conformed to the demonic world. Cults also facilitate demonization by initiating members through some kind of process that gives permission for demonic engagement, often without the participant knowing what is going on.

A curse of cults can be activated by an ancestor, thus affecting future generations without their awareness. The evidence for such a curse in the current generation often includes an inclination toward spiritual error and a resistance to the gospel message. Should such a person accept Christ, he or she will encounter spiritual interference on a regular basis. Worship, prayer, Bible study, or any expression of faith will be hindered for people who have inherited the effects of their forebear's cult involvement.

It can be difficult to determine the actual belief system of a cultish group. This is because what you see on the outside may only be the public face, while under the surface, abominations lurk in the dark. Naturally, cult teachings that are expected to stir up a reaction in outsiders will remain part of the private, esoteric knowledge, while only the more broadly palatable aspects of the belief system will be presented to the outside world. For example, Scientology has a certain exoteric (public) image that has been cast in the image of the Hollywood stars who have become members, but its far-fetched esoteric (private) codes leak out only occasionally. The same can be said about the Mormons, who make every effort to present themselves to the public as just another traditional Christian denomination populated with happy families.

When a person becomes a member of a cult, he or she will learn about the hidden belief system progressively, over time. In many groups, neophytes will not be aware of any higher state of initiation. As they become more involved, their knowledge about such things will evolve. For this reason, cult-related curses must always be broken according to the degree of involvement on the part of the cult member. You can't ask people to confess and renounce beliefs that they did not ever know about.

To the average person who just had a couple of Mormons or Jehovah's Witnesses knock on the door and go through their little pitch, their visitors appear to be only well-intentioned, if unsophisticated, door-to-door evangelists. Even newcomers who begin to attend services will find that nothing alarming takes place and that many aspects of the routines resemble those of many Protestant churches or Sunday schools. Only after deeper involvement would someone find out, for example, about the Mormons's binding temple oaths or their belief in the brotherhood of Jesus and Lucifer—or about the Jehovah's Witnesses's faulty biblical scholarship and out-of-context interpretations.

OVERVIEW OF CURSED CULTS

In general terms, the reason that cult involvement invites a curse is that its ultimate intent is Luciferian—satanic and against Jesus Christ. In many cults, Jesus is portrayed as merely an exceptionally good man, and the Trinity is unheard of or reinterpreted. Freemasons, for instance, tend to relate to God only as a "supreme being." Often in a cult, salvation or its equivalent can be achieved by human effort and good works, with the recommended works matching the teachings of the group. Think of Unity or Baha'i. Or salvation itself may not be the goal of the group. Some (even some of the better-known groups such as Scientology) promote belief in reincarnation.

With many beliefs that are in direct opposition to the Bible, cultish groups dehumanize the individual believer and make them subservient. Anyone who thinks for himself or herself is suspected of disloyalty. Remember the news reports in recent years that revealed the servile mentality of the women in the FLDS (Fundamentalist Church of Jesus Christ of Latter-Day Saints). Members of cults experience a high degree of personal oversight.

Often God is defined narrowly, and deviations from accepted nomenclature are not tolerated. For example, Jehovah's Witnesses insist that Jehovah is the only proper name for God, claiming that it dates back to Old Testament times. They ignore the fact that Greek and Hebrew scholars report no instances of the name in the original Scriptures and that it appeared only with William Tyndale's 1525 rendering of the Hebrew consonants YHWH ("Yahweh") in his English translation of the Bible.

KINDS OF CULTS THAT CAUSE CURSES

Starting in the 1960s, the number of cults with an active presence in the Western world increased greatly. Even if God sent massive revival today, it would take us four more generations to undo the mess of curses that have been activated in the past generation, four more generations to kick out all the yogis and the gurus, the witches and the Satanists, and all the evil they have brought on this country. According to the principles of Exodus 20 and 34, as stated earlier in this book, four generations is the minimum life of a curse and the least amount of time necessary to completely undo the societal effect of a curse.

Cults that cause curses fall into four categories or types: (1) mystical cults, (2) pagan cults, (3) cults of spiritualism, and (4) cults of occultism. These categories are not firmly separated from one another, but they are useful for purposes of explanation and, therefore, for freeing people from their bondage.

Mystical cults: I define mysticism as anything that promotes an altered state of consciousness by means of meditation. What is it about mysticism that leads to demonic bondage and curses? First of all, any time people put aside their minds and surrender their volition, they open themselves to other forces, most of which are not friendly. To get in touch with the "universal consciousness" or sense the "primordial vibration of the divine word" allows the entrance of malign influences. When they are resting in a nonassertive state, people do not resist whatever spiritual power comes their way.

I am constantly running into people who somewhat innocently experimented with yoga, not understanding that simply by assuming the postures they tuned themselves in to the spirit world and lined themselves up with an occult system of philosophy. This is even more likely to happen as yoga becomes accepted as part of the mainstream, even within evangelical churches. Ignoring the fact that for millennia yoga principles have been used to facilitate demonization, yoga practitioners give implicit consent to deception and bondage.

You will notice that mystical cults tend to define God in non-theistic terms, without moral accountability. People open themselves up to curses when they become involved in groups that promote openness to the spiritual realm without establishing objective, transcendent moral accountability—in other words, without endorsing the sovereignty and supremacy of a living, active God.

Within the ranks of mystical cults are those who advocate communication with the spirits of departed "ascended masters," such as certain I AM cults. While in an altered state of consciousness, people pick up demons from whatever more "highly evolved," deceased individual they choose to get in touch with. I have found that certain standard demonic names pop up repeatedly in the experience of those of us who pray regularly for people who have been involved in the Hindu and Hindu-influenced cults. Brahma, Vishnu, Shiva (Siva), and Kali are just a few of the demon gods that accompany Eastern cult curses. Each demon comes with a different kind of curse.

Almost universally, reincarnation undergirds mystical belief systems. As people seek to get in touch with whoever they may have been in the past, mimicking demons will manifest through them, purporting to carry knowledge of some long-gone personage. As they pursue information, the seekers pick up demonic curses.

Although the people who look for "enlightenment" may sincerely desire to seek more of God and to learn more about themselves, the sad result is that they become enmeshed in a deceptive web of demonic curses from which it can become more difficult to escape with each progressive experimentation (e.g., Transcendental Meditation, Tantra, Qigong, Tai Chi).

Pagan cults: With ancient pagan religions such as Wicca and witchcraft, as well as any kind of neo-paganism, rituals are central. Rituals involve actual contact with evil powers. They entail compliance with an established protocol to conjure occult powers as part of a ceremony.

Many of the rituals purposefully invoke curses and summon demons. Therefore, when identifying specific curses and breaking them in cases in which someone has had direct involvement with a pagan religion, it will be helpful to find out what rituals have been undertaken in the past. In many cases, gods and goddesses, who are demons in disguise, will be invoked by name.

Followers of pagan religions generally worship the forces of nature. This is not the same as acknowledging the Creator of the earth in worship. Replacing God as the object of worship with one of His creations constitutes demonic veneration. Such a pantheistic approach to the natural features of the world essentially connects people to the demons that lie behind the pagan belief system. Summonings may invoke real demons, and with each demon comes a curse connected to the invocation.

Paganism almost always includes attempts to communicate with invisible entities from the "other side." Guess what those entities usually turn out to be?

Spiritualism: Spiritualism is an outgrowth of spiritism, which is a pagan practice far outside of the Judeo-Christian tradition. Largely devoted to communicating with the dead (necromancy), spiritualism appeals especially to people who have lost a loved one. Those who communicate with the spirits of the dead consort with demons in the process.

Necromancy is specifically forbidden in the Old Testament Book of Deuteronomy:

> *There shall not be found among you anyone who makes his son or his daughter pass through the fire, or one who practices witchcraft, or a soothsayer, or one who interprets omens, or a sorcerer, or one who conjures spells, or a medium, or a spiritist, or one who calls up the dead. For all who do these things are an abomination to the Lord...* (Deuteronomy 18:10-12).

Originally, the violation of God's commands brought down a sentence of capital punishment, which was considered commensurate with the seriousness of the violation and an immediate manifestation of the curse. Since the time of Moses, God has drawn a line of demarcation, which people are not supposed to cross. He has taken pains to warn His people, "Don't go there. Don't do that." People ignore Him at their peril.

When sorcery is involved (even seemingly simple and harmless party entertainments such as playing with Ouija boards) the curses attached to the practice of sorcery will fall on people. How much more will intentional engagement with tarot card reading, horoscopes, or pursuit of any kind of psychic phenomena bring curses into the life of an individual?

The curses laid out in Deuteronomy 27-29 still apply today. They have not been outmoded or superseded over time. In summary:

> *All these curses shall come upon you and pursue and overtake you, until you are destroyed, because you did not obey the voice of the Lord your God, to keep His commandments and His statutes which He commanded you. And they shall be upon you for a sign and a wonder, and on your descendants forever* (Deuteronomy 28:45-46).

The very demons that impersonate the spirits of the dead try to lead people to believe that death is a fiction, and yet those who invoke such spirits run the significant risk of premature death, preceded by illness, accidents, and other types of suffering. Spiritualism is far from innocuous.

Occultism: The word occult comes from a Latin root that means "to cover up" or "conceal." Occult practices are motivated by a belief in hidden or mysterious powers and the hope of subjecting those powers to human control. As you can surmise, most of the types of cults I have mentioned above could be termed "occult," because they attempt to lift the veil to the unknown, while using secret techniques that can open the human soul to demons.

Some of these techniques give practitioners neurosensory feedback that promotes a desired state of mind. Others, such as induced trance states, alter the perception of reality in hopes of obtaining spiritual guidance.

Curse Breaking

A common practice of these kinds of cults is to separate the contemporary involvement from the distinctive historical roots of false religions and witchcraft. This is done with practices as diverse as yoga and acupuncture. Various healing modalities, such as Reiki and therapeutic touch, may seem harmless, but the occult faith of the practitioner and the underlying belief system of the technique may pollute the process with a curse. For example, I have known Christians who fell prey to demonic oppression when they were treated by chiropractors who followed the Chinese meridian theory to treat pain by using pressure to change the way that qi (life energy) flows in the body, seeking to balance the ying and the yang, polar opposites in Taoism. One woman I ministered to was tormented by a curse placed on her by a non-Christian Chinese dentist who treated her gum disease with herbs that had been ritually concocted. The danger in performing or receiving any therapy that is based on a false religion or demonic philosophy is that it taps into occult powers, whether or not the "healer" or the recipient desires such an outcome. This opens the door to whatever curses are attached to that particular belief system. Demons do not need to ask permission to enter if someone has already invited them in by opening the door.

Divination, according to the Bible, is an abomination. (See Leviticus 19:26, 31; Deuteronomy 18:9-14.) The prophet Isaiah had much to say about what God thought about such occult practices:

> *You, Lord, have abandoned your people, the house of Jacob. They are full of superstitions from the East; they practice divination like the Philistines and clasp hands with pagans. Their land is full of silver and gold; there is no end to their treasures. Their land is full of horses; there is no end to their chariots. Their land is full of idols; they bow down to the work of their hands, to what their fingers have made. So man will be brought low and mankind humbled—do not forgive them* (Isaiah 2:6-9 NIV).

Even such things as consulting a horoscope out of curiosity or calling a psychic hotline are not minor matters in God's eyes. Anyone who has dabbled in occult practices, not to mention those who have deliberately committed themselves to the devil by means of arcane, evil rituals, can only find freedom from bondage by sincerely repenting and refraining from further contact with such things. With help from fellow Christians, the curses can be broken.

SPIRITS ASSOCIATED WITH "DOCTRINES OF DEMONS"

The apostle Paul advised the younger man Timothy as follows:

Now the Spirit expressly says that in latter times some will depart from the faith, giving heed to deceiving spirits and doctrines of demons, speaking lies in hypocrisy, having their own conscience seared with a hot iron.... Reject profane and old wives' fables, and exercise yourself toward godliness (1 Timothy 4:1-2, 7).

Who are these demons who promulgate false doctrines? One fairly obvious one is the demon of deception or lies. Another is the demon of blasphemy. Often you will find demons who go by the names Antichrist or Lucifer or one of the biblical demon-gods, such as Moloch (to whom people used to sacrifice their children) or Baal.

In any religious system that is based on lies, you can expect to find a lying spirit of some kind. Because cults, even cults that use Jesus's name, do not hold Him higher than other spirits and forces, they point people toward the fallen angel, Lucifer. Thus, Lucifer is at the top of false religious systems, often aided by Baal because he goes far back in religious history as the chief god of false religious systems. You will remember Elijah's confrontation with the prophets of Baal on Mt. Carmel (see 1 Kings 18). Under the rule of Ahab and Jezebel, the prophets of Baal were powerful, and they stood in opposition to true Judaism.

Speaking of Jezebel, you will often run into a demon by the same name when you are dealing with a false religious system. That is because false and evil directives so frequently trace to that evil spirit (see Revelation 2:20-23).

Breaking the curses of cults does not so much involve dealing with spirits of, say, anger or murder or rejection, as is the case with more personal curses. Instead, you will find spirits in the categories I have just mentioned: Deception, Blasphemy, Antichrist, and Lucifer.

HOW TO REMOVE A CULT-RELATED CURSE

When a cult-related curse has been suspected or identified, one of the first steps to freedom should be the renouncing of all soul ties with the leader or the founder of that cult. An emotional or spiritual link to that person almost always exists, and it keeps followers under an invisible thumb.

Mormonism provides one of the best examples of what I am describing. When confronted by outsiders with any inconsistencies in their doctrines, Mormons have been taught to make a statement such as this: "By the burning in my bosom, I know that Joseph Smith, Jr. is the prophet of God." They profess a link with the founder of the Latter Day Saint movement, or Mormon Church. In a similar way, people from Eastern religions have paid obeisance to some guru or to that guru's lineage. Those who have practiced transcendental meditation, for example, have not only paid homage to the late Maharishi Mahesh Yogi, but they have made themselves subject to his spiritual master, Swami Brahmananda Saraswati.

Depending upon the religion or cult, an adherent who wishes to get free from all curses must shake off the demons of the founders by renouncing all ties to them, by name. It is always helpful to do this in the company of other Christians, to fulfill the teachings of Christ, that a prayer is heard and answered when there is spiritual agreement.

> *Again I say to you that if two of you agree on earth concerning anything that they ask, it will be done for them by My Father in heaven. For where two or three are gathered together in My name, I am there in the midst of them* (Matthew 18:19-20).

The next step would be to renounce doctrinal creeds and confessions. Followers of one branch of Japanese Nichiren Buddhism, for example, who have been chanting the Diamoku (a worship formula said to put one in tune with the universe), will have to not only stop chanting it and destroy their written copies of it, but also specifically renounce the chant itself, because it is a creedal statement. Men who come out of Freemasonry (which we will discuss in more detail in the next chapter) must renounce all the blood oaths that they have entered into and every secret ceremony, rite, and ritual, because these utterances have demonic curses attached to them.

Renouncing everything can get complicated, particularly when someone has spent a lot of time as a member of one of these groups, because the bondage only gets more extensive with time. It is as if the devil builds this massive internal architecture of evil. This architecture resembles that of a large building. When you approach it, you see only an edifice. But as you come inside, you discover that it is much more than a shell. You will find various rooms with different purposes. You will see people in some of those rooms who are doing different kinds of things. You see a plan at work, an infrastructure within the architecture. This is what happens when the devil establishes a curse. It is up to us to identify the things that stem from the evil curses of the devil so that we can deal with them. To the best of our ability, we need to recall the language and aspects of the ceremonies in order to renounce them and place them under the blood of Christ.

One special ritual would be marriage. If two people have been married under the auspices of, say, the Mormon Church, they would need to renounce their Mormon vows and make new ones in a Christian church. I am not suggesting that they should renounce their marriage itself or that they should divorce and get remarried. The civil aspect of their union is intact. But the Mormon marriage vows commit the couple to be wedded for time and all eternity, which represents an eternal bonding to the curses behind the belief system.

Another important aspect when breaking the curses of cults is the renunciation of any spirit guides or revelators of the religion. Almost every group has some connection to a revelator—some person to whom the so-called truth of the religion was transmitted. For Mormons, this would be the angel Moroni, by whom founder Joseph Smith, Jr. claimed to have been visited on many occasions. Jehovah's Witnesses should renounce the sect's false archangel Michael. A Muslim would need to renounce the supposed archangel Gabriel, who they believe brought the Koran to Mohammed. A devotee of Eckankar would need to renounce Sugmad, and so forth.

It can take many keys to unlock and break a cultish curse. The more keys a person uses, the more effectively the curse can be broken. One key would be getting rebaptized if baptism was a part of the requirements of the cult. I encourage people to be rebaptized even if they are coming out of a Christian-seeming cult such as Jesus Only groups, because their baptisms do not follow the Trinitarian formula. The previous baptism is not going to keep somebody out of Heaven, but I believe that it will be an emotional and spiritual hindrance to their growth in the Christian faith and in their freedom from the curse of the cult.

Other keys include reversing particular vows and oaths, renouncing affirmations and confessions, and discarding books of teachings. Any object or codified belief system will be a means by which the tentacles of the cult can maintain some sort of grip on the person. The last section of this book contains useful information for further curse breaking.

FINDING GOD'S GRACE ANEW

God is endlessly patient and merciful.

> *The Lord is not slow in keeping his promise, as some understand slowness. Instead he is patient with you, not wanting anyone to perish, but everyone to come to repentance* (2 Peter 3:9 NIV).

In spite of our ignorance and foolishness, He looks after us. Theologians call it the "common grace" of God. Without this grace, surely every one of us would have perished in our sin, swallowed up by demonic curses. That is good news.

Yet people who enter into cults end up kissing God's common grace goodbye for the most part. They will walk under it for some time, "for He makes His sun rise on the evil and on the good, and sends rain on the just and on the unjust" (Matt. 5:45). But one of the deadliest things about cults, the occult, mysticism, paganism, and the New Age is that they are specific forms of spiritual rebellion. Dedicated participants are actively repudiating the grace of God.

Although the Christian community promotes the idea that all sins are the same because every sin separates us from God, that view ignores the degree to which sin will affect people in terms of their potential for demonization. Curses are guaranteed to follow people's involvement in non-Christian religions or alternative groups, making them (and their families) vulnerable to spiritual entities that God wants us to avoid at any cost.

God extends His grace to anyone who returns to Him. The apostle Paul, writing to people whose culture was saturated with paganism and false gods, said,

> *Do not offer the parts of your body to sin, as instruments of wickedness, but rather offer yourselves to God, as those who have been brought from death to life; and offer the parts of your body to him as instruments of righteousness. For sin shall not be your master, because you are not under law, but under grace* (Romans 6:13-14 NIV).

As He shines His light into darkness, may those who are in bondage to curses of cults follow His light until they are free indeed.

ENDNOTES

1. Bob Larson, *Larson's Book of World Religions and Alternative Spirituality* (Wheaton, IL: Tyndale, 2004), 16.
2. Ibid., 19.

Chapter 6

CURSES OF CLANDESTINE CULTS

I was ministering to a young African American man I will call Malik. Suddenly his voice changed from being clear and pleasant to raspy and vicious. As two of my assistants took hold of his arms, I said, "I come against you, evil spirit, in the name of Jesus. I oppose what you are trying to do to this man. I bind and rebuke you in Jesus's name."

Leave me alone! he hissed in my face. My helpers had to tighten their grip.

"I think you are an intruder where you do not belong."

Leave me alone. You have no right, he snapped.

"What is the right?"

I was welcomed.

"Welcomed? By this man or his ancestors?"

Both.

"Your name?"

Murder.

"Murder, go to torment. I want to talk to this man." The host of this evil spirit relaxed, and I put my arm around his shoulder. "What's your first name, sir?"

"Malik," he replied in a normal tone of voice.

"Malik, how old are you?"

"Thirty."

"What is the worst thing that ever happened in your life, Malik?"

"Abuse." His answers were short, but not curt. He did not really want to elaborate.

"Abuse from whom?"

"My father."

"What kind of abuse?"

"Physical. He beat me bad."

"How bad?"

"He broke some bones."

It was becoming clear that the spirit of Murder had come into him as a boy, when he was so frightfully beaten by his father. But as I looked into his eyes, I could see something else, so I laid my large cross on his forehead. Immediately, Malik's normal voice disappeared and the raspy voice returned.

Get that thing off of me! He barked through clenched teeth.

I left the cross where it was. "How many generations have you afflicted this man and his ancestors?"

A long time.

"I know you have been there a long time, but that is not the answer I'm looking for. How many generations?"

Malik started thrashing about and fighting his restraint, and the ugly voice came back with the answer: Fourteen...Fourteen...Fourteen. The demon's voice grew louder with each declaration of the number of generations this curse had been tormenting Malik's family line.

"I want to know what happened fourteen generations ago?"

I was welcomed.

"By whom? His ancestors?"

Yes.

"In a ceremony?"

Yes.

"With blood?"

Yes.

"Human or animal?"

Both. Both. Both. He began to struggle again.

"You are appointed to judgment this night, and the fourteen generations have come to an end."

No! Not my time!

"Oh, yes, it is your time. I commanded the foul spirit to repeat after me: "We lift the curse…"

We lift the curssssse…

"…from him."

The evil voice growled with malice.

"I put the wrath of God on you, seven times greater than all of all the generations that you tormented."

The demon growled at the severity of the judgment, inarticulate with wails of despair and fury. Then, I switched to my next tactic. "Malik, come to me for a minute. I want you to repeat after me. Say, 'I, Malik…'"

"I, Malik…"

"…break the ancient curse…"

"…break the ancient curse…"

"…of destruction and witchcraft…"

"…of destruction and witchcraft…"

"…that came from my ancestors in Africa fourteen generations ago."

"…that came from my ancestors in Africa fourteen generations ago."

"The curse is broken. Now we'll get rid of this evil spirit."

I have the right to stay here, the demon snarled in response.

"No, you don't. No, you don't."

Yesss, The voice hissed. He likes what he's doing!

"No, he really doesn't. Say, 'I, Murder…'"

No! I am not leaving! Bucking and kicking.

"Say, 'I, Murder…'"

I, Murder (with struggle)…

"…give up…. give up…"

Can't!

"Say, '…every right to this man…'"

…every right to this man…

"…and his family…."

…and his family…This was torture for the spirit, and he could hardly speak at all. Yet he complied.

"All of us…"

Malik's eyes got big, and the harsh voice spat it out: All of us…

"…receive…" (I could only give him one or two words at a time, because it was all he could do to speak.)

…receive…

"…the judgment…"

…the judgment…

"…of Almighty God."

…of Almighty God.

"And we all…"

(Over objections) And we all…

"…go…"

…go…

"…to…"

…to…

"…the pit!"

Along with unintelligible sounds of objection, he repeated:…go to the pit…Awrghhh!

Immediately, Malik straightened up with an almost-smile on his face. "Hallelujah!" I said. "Jesus did this for you. Jesus receives the glory."

Malik threw both arms up in the air and began to jump up and down with joy, shouting and clapping.

THE PROBLEM WITH BLOOD OATHS

That was one nasty demon. African demons are like that. When you tap into African ancestral demons that carry those types of curses, you have your hands full. Fourteen generations, going back to his ancestors in Africa. And at the beginning, a blood covenant. The fact that in this particular case the blood was human and animal made the curse more powerful and more difficult to break.

As I have checked back through our film archives to find other sessions such as this one, I have found that every single one of these ancient demons came because of curses. You can get rid of other demons without breaking the curse. But to get rid of one of these bad ones, the curse must first be broken.

Some dark night way back in time, another young man who was one of Malik's many-great-grandfathers participated in a covert ceremony. In all probability, he wanted to have more strength to fight his enemies or the skill to be a better hunter. The details are completely lost to us now. Secret ceremonies invoke formidable forces of evil, and blood-saturated imprecations are only part of the clandestine rites that inevitably invoke curses on the participants.

CLANDESTINE CULTS ON AMERICAN SOIL

While any of us may well encounter a curse inherited from someone's ancestor on a faraway continent, the most likely source of curses associated with clandestine cults is right in our midst. Almost every city of any size hosts more than one. These organizations present a harmless public face, often appearing to be social organizations that are not particularly religious. Looks can be deceiving.

Besides the fact that they all maintain a strict wall of secrecy around many of their beliefs, teachings, and ceremonies, all of them share certain characteristics that bring about curses. For one, they nearly always have a connection to someone who was spiritually deceptive in promoting or founding the religion or fraternal group. Sometimes, possibly often, that connection extends back to previous generations of the original founder.

That is one reason, for example, to classify Mormonism as a clandestine cult. Most people have heard of their founder, Joseph Smith, Jr., but how much do we know about him? His father, Joseph, Sr., was an occultist. Like many others in the early years of the nineteenth century, he was a treasure-seeker, always looking for some lost cache. He would take his son along with him when he went looking for the booty of Captain Kidd. He would try to find the lost treasure by means of divination, most frequently using something called seer stones or peepstones that he would put over his eyes and peer through.

Joseph Smith, Jr. grew up with this as part of his experience. In fact, he claimed to have translated the unknown Egyptian hieroglyphic texts that became the Book of Mormon by means of peepstones, after having obtained inscribed golden plates from the angel Moroni.

Another typical characteristic of a clandestine cult is the adherence to false doctrines, usually imperfectly understood by outsiders because of secrecy. Enough about them tends to leak out, however, to recognize their fallacies. Adherence to false doctrines implicates members in the active refutation of the truth (even while they are likely to feel that they have attained a higher truth). As we have seen from the Old Testament Scriptures, adherence to false doctrines draws down an inevitable spiritual curse.

Often the false doctrines lead to outright blasphemy, which is a curse in and of itself. Many Mormons, for example, have been taught that God himself was once procreated in another world, and that now humans may aspire to the status of procreator. In other words, Adam did the right thing when he ate of the forbidden fruit, because it made him capable of fathering the human race. Men and women are potential father and mother gods. The book of Mormon states: "Adam fell that men might be." A famous Mormon aphorism declares, "As man now is, God once was; as God now is, man may become." This right to godhead is not earned by the grace of Jesus Christ, but rather by being a good Mormon, faithful to the Temple.

In the following pages, let's take a look at some specific cults that are clandestine in nature.

FREEMASONRY

When we were shooting our reality television show, we went to New York City to film the final exorcism of the episode, and we were looking for a church to serve as the filming venue. The production staff got on the phone and called six evangelical churches in the immediate area, and they all said no. They kept trying, calling more churches. After they had reached the bottom of their list, the department head called me to report. "Reverend Bob, we have called everyone, and all of them said no—except at the very end we found someone who will let us come inside and film."

"Where?" I asked.

"In the largest Masonic lodge in New York City." I couldn't believe it.

Soon we were walking into a place that ordinarily we would be barred from entering, and we were allowed go into the most sacrosanct parts of it. We passed through the massive, solid bronze doors that were over 20 feet tall, and we saw a sign advertising some festivity. Next to it was a pentagram (it was the two-points-up version of the five-pointed star used by Masons and also Satanists). A caption read, "With faith, all things are possible," which is a corruption of the verse of the Bible: "With God all things are possible" (Matt. 19:26).

We walked on in to the inner sanctum, and we saw the heavy chair of the Worshipful Master, behind a podium. Above it was the Masonic symbol, composed of the stonemason's tools of a square and a compass, with a capital G inside. This letter G is supposed to stand for the word "geometry," and also for "Grand Architect," or God. In all likelihood it stands for a whole lot more than that, none of it good. So I decided to anoint the thing. I climbed up on the arms of the chair and reached up as high as I could in order to anoint it with oil in the name of the Father, Son, and Holy Spirit. Then I got down into the chair and sat right down. It is not that I have an ambition to be the Worshipful Master of a Masonic temple, but I know that the Spirit of Jesus dwells in me, and I thought this would be one of the first times Jesus had ever had a chance to sit in what is essentially the chair of Lucifer.

Much has been written and said about Freemasonry, which has often been a controversial group. Its obscure and allegorical origins go back centuries in Europe. In most places, it is a fraternal (male-only) organization. The best-known offshoots for women and girls in the United States are known as the Order of the Eastern Star and the International Order of the Rainbow for Girls. Rituals play a central role in gatherings of members, and although the organization does not identify itself as a religious group, terminology and symbols borrowed from many religions can be found at every level.

Who is God here? Masons acknowledge a "Supreme Architect," but this deity is purposely ambiguous. At the time of his initiation, a man must declare his faith in this supreme being, but he is never required to say what god he worships, if any. False religions are integrated throughout the Masonic experience.

Curse Breaking

The main room of the New York lodge has a ceiling that appears to be over 30 feet high. On one side, we saw four massive plaques, each three or four feet square (hard to estimate because they were so high), and each one of them carried a depiction and an inscription. One read, "The Mythology of Judaism," and others read, "The Mythology of the Greeks," "The Mythology of the Egyptians," and "The Mythology of the Assyrians." Those four major religious systems were represented there, but we did not see a single cross in the room. The place has a decidedly religious feel to it, but it is not the kind of spirituality that I want to get close to.

In Chapters 4 and 5, I mentioned the extreme negative significance of oaths and vows. Masons are known for their death oath, spoken aloud by initiates, which seals the spiritual curse that comes with Entered Apprenticeship. Here is a sampling of the wording they repeat when they take the oath:

> I, _____, of my own free will and accord, in the presence of Almighty God, and this Worshipful Lodge of Fellow Craft Masons,...do hereby and hereon [the oath may or may not be taken with one hand on a Bible] most solemnly promise and swear, in addition to my former obligation, that I will not give the secrets of the degree of a Fellow Craft Mason to any one of an inferior degree, nor to any other being in the known world, except it to be a true and lawful brother or brethren Fellow Craft Masons, within the body of a just and lawfully constituted lodge of such; and not unto him nor unto them, whom I shall hear so to be, but unto him and them only whom I shall find so to be after strict trial and due examination or lawful information. Furthermore do I promise and swear that I will not wrong this lodge nor a brother of this degree to the value of two cents, knowingly, myself, nor suffer it to be done by others if in my power to prevent it. Furthermore do I promise and swear that I will support the Constitution of the Grand Lodge of the United States, and of the Grand Lodge of this State, under which this lodge is held, and conform to all

the by-laws, rules, and regulations of this or any other lodge of which I may at any time hereafter become a member, as far as in my power. Furthermore, do I promise and swear that I will obey all regular signs and summonses given, handed, sent, or thrown to me by the hand of a brother Fellow Craft Mason, or from the body of a just and lawfully constituted lodge of such, provided that it be within the length of my cable-tow, or square and angle of my work. Furthermore, do I promise and swear that I will be aiding and assisting all poor and Penniless brethren Fellow Crafts, their widows and orphans, wheresoever disposed round the globe, they applying to me as such, as far as in my power without injuring myself or family. To all which I do most solemnly and sincerely promise and swear without the least hesitation, mental reservation, or self evasion of mind in me whatever; binding myself under no less penalty than to have my left breast torn open and my heart and vitals taken from thence and thrown over my left shoulder and carried into the valley of Jehosaphat, there to become a prey to the wild beasts of the field, and vulture of the air, if ever I should prove willfully guilty of violating any part of this my solemn oath or obligation of a Fellow Craft Mason; so help me God, and keep me steadfast in the due performance of the same. [This oath is recited blindfolded, and the candidate has been partially stripped and bound with a cable-tie (tow). Afterward the candidate receives a special handgrip and passwords.]

You can see why it is called a death oath: "...binding myself under no less penalty than to have my left breast torn open and my heart and vitals taken...to become prey to the wild beasts of the field, and vulture of the air." Even when people do not take it seriously, this oath is binding—and it is only one among many. Others are even more self-suicidal, declaring their willingness to have their throats slit from ear to ear. (At this the new Free-mason is instructed to slash his hand across his throat, mimicking the act of murder.) Masons will argue, "Well, these oaths are just symbolic. They are not meant to be taken literally." However, why would anyone want to put himself under such incredible judgment if there is really nothing to it?

If you read carefully through the lofty-sounding wording, you can see that the oath-taker swears higher allegiance to his fellow Masons than to any others. This means that every Christian who claims also to be a mason has sworn to take care of his fellow Masons first, before his Christian brethren.

You can understand why some of the strongest curses you will ever encounter are Freemason curses. Besides premature death, among the specific curses uttered under oath are curses of disease, suffering, family strife and troubles, and sexual violation. I have found that, in cases of unexplained barrenness or repeated miscarriage and in serious cases of molestation or pedophilia, a curse of Freemasonry was to blame. Sometimes such aspects of the curse fall on the Mason's own family and other times it has been inherited by their children. Often the descendants of Freemasons suffer a series of accidents, serious physical injuries, strange illnesses, and odd misfortunes. In one case, several grandchildren of a Mason were electrocuted. Another family, descended from a 32nd degree Mason, had one child with Down Syndrome, another who molested his sister, and a third child who had an eye poked out. Could pure coincidence explain such horrible tragedies all in the children of one family?

Whole books have been written about the cult of Freemasonry, which has influenced many other sects and organizations in the course of its history. I trust that this brief description is adequate to convince you that this clandestine cult has engendered, and continues to engender, countless curses and unnecessary suffering.

MORMONS

One of the religious sects that has roots in Freemasonry is the Mormon Church, also known as the Church of Jesus Christ of Latter-Day Saints (LDS). LDS founder Joseph Smith, Jr., joined the Masonic lodge in Nauvoo, Illinois, as a young man and introduced a number of death-dealing phrases and oaths into Mormon dedication ceremonies that bore almost word-for-word similarity to the oaths of the Freemasons. Until relatively recently, Mormons's vows used the same penalties in their endowment ceremonies—rituals that prepare them to become the royalty and priesthood of life after death—as the Masons. Even after the gory words were taken out of the ceremony, they still retained the penalty gesture for a while, a slashing motion across their throats and stomachs.[1] The existence of such explicit death penalties only underlines the clandestine nature of the Mormon devotion. The endowment ceremonies still take place behind closed doors, as do many other key practices.

Even though adherence varies from place to place, false doctrines such as the following persist, providing fertile soil for the sowing of curses:

- Heaven has three tiers for heathen, non-Mormon Christians, and those with sealed marriages whose earthly matrimonial unions will endure forever.

- The state of women is inferior to that of men.

- The US Constitution is divinely inspired.

- Special undergarments protect wearers, both male and female, from both temptation and physical dangers.

- Proxy baptisms ensure the salvation of people already dead, whether they are saints or sinners. (Thus the Mormon preoccupation with genealogy.)

- Satan is Jesus's and Adam's rebellious spirit brother.

- Interracial marriages are disallowed. (Church policy has only gradually become less anti-black in general after church leaders received a "revelation" from God.)

In addition, an apocalyptic mentality is cultivated in the church, and members are urged to store up food to prepare for times of famine.

The Mormon Church believes in the gifts of the Spirit, but as one who uses the gift of discernment of spirits on a regular basis, I find their apparent methods to be unorthodox, to say the least, because it involves shaking the hand of another person (or possibly an angel's hand or a demon's hand) to see what happens. Joseph Smith's advice, preserved in section 129 of the Mormon text, The Doctrine and Covenants, is to test supposed messengers from heaven by this means.[2]

The belief system is so complex and confusing, even to Mormons, that many members simply give preference to the rites and ideas that they find easier to understand. Nevertheless, anyone who has Mormonism in his or her family history, and certainly anyone who has been a member of the Mormon Church, should do a thorough "spiritual housecleaning," breaking the demonic curses that accompany these many ill-conceived beliefs and rituals.

CAMARADERIE CULTS

Now we will turn our attention to three organizations that are representative of what I call "camaraderie cults": the Knights of Columbus, the Elks, and the Woodmen of the World. Other such groups exist, but we can learn the basics about them by taking a look at these three.

Founded in the United States over 130 years ago and now international in membership, the Knights of Columbus is a fraternal organization with ties to the Catholic Church. Group members perform charitable acts that range from disaster relief to funding scholarships. The organization was started in Connecticut by a very devout Irish-American priest as a kind of mutual benefit society to help out fellow immigrant Catholics, most of whom were poor. The founder sought the benefits of a fraternal organization for the Catholic men in his parish, but the Catholic Church was (and still is) rightfully opposed to Freemasonry and other fraternal orders. So they founded their own organization.

The problem is that, in an effort to strengthen their appeal to potential members, they ended up adopting some of the same secret practices as the Freemasons. I am not saying that the Knights of Columbus is an evil organization or that they have perpetrated as many curses as the Freemasons. Far from it. They do a lot of philanthropic good. However, I am wary of organizations that bury their rituals and oaths in secrecy because, by its very nature, this kind of clandestine activity allows an opportunity for evil to enter in.

Another organization, the Benevolent Protective Order of Elks (BPOE), commonly known simply as the Elks Lodge or the Elks, started out in the late nineteenth century as a social club. At first they called themselves the Jolly Corks, because they were a private drinking establishment. They adopted a fraternal service orientation when needs arose among the families of their members. For a long time, membership was restricted to men only; today women too may be members. Membership is restricted to United States citizens over the age of 21 who believe in God.

Many of the original members of the Jolly Corks were theatrical actors in New York City. One of them had been a member of a centuries-old fraternal organization in England known as the Royal and Antediluvian Order of Buffaloes, and he imported a number of their rituals to the new organization that became the Order of Elks. (I once did an exorcism on a man from Trinidad whose father was a British member of the Buffaloes and had passed demons and a curse to his son. In fact, the exorcism began when the man attempted to assault me and threatened to kill me. He had an animal-like demeanor, like that of a raging buffalo.)

One of the ritual traditions of the Elks is called "the 11 o'clock toast." The eleventh hour of the day had acquired an almost mystical significance over the years because so many communities had a "lights out at eleven" policy. This toast is intended to honor the departed members of the organization, but can end up essentially communicating with the dead. This is the wording used by the Elks:

> You have heard the tolling of eleven strokes. This is to remind
> us that with Elks, the hour of eleven has a tender significance.
> Wherever an Elk may roam, whatever his lot in life may be,
> when this hour falls upon the dial of night the great heart of
> Elkdom swells and throbs. It is the golden hour of recollection,
> the homecoming of those who wander, the mystic roll call
> of those who will come no more. Living or dead, an Elk is
> never forgotten, never forsaken. Morning and noon may pass

him by, the light of day sink heedlessly in the west, but ere the shadows of midnight shall fall, the chimes of memory will be pealing forth the friendly message—"TO OUR ABSENT MEMBERS."[3]

The Elks, like the Freemasons, established their own burial ceremonies and plots. These are no longer being developed, but in connection with the burials of dedicated Elks members, the motto of the Elks was altered from "Once an Elk, Always an Elk" to "Once an Elk, Eternally an Elk." Dozens of cemeteries across the nation contain Elk statuary and tombstones.[4]

Speaking of tombstones, old cemeteries in several states often contain stone replicas of tree stumps. These mark the graves of deceased members of the fraternal order known as Woodmen of the World. The organization began to identify graves in this way in about 1880 and stopped in about 1935.[5]

Today, the organization is best known for its large private insurance company, based in Omaha, Nebraska. That city is where the Woodmen of the World was founded by a man named Joseph Cullen Root, who has been termed "America's most prolific founder of fraternal benefit societies":

> Root held a firm conviction that Freemasonry and other fraternal organizations had an important role to play in the promotion of human welfare. Thus, he sought light in Masonry…[advancing upward through the various degrees or levels.] He also held membership in the Knights Templar, the Knights of Pythias, and the Independent Order of Odd Fellows. [Pythia was the priestess at the ancient Greek Oracle of Delphi, and functioned under the control of a snake-like spirit, to utter supposed prophesies. Those in spiritual warfare ministries recognize this evil force as the demon Python.]
>
> Root's earliest experience with fraternal benefit societies included involvement in the Iowa Legion of Honor, the Ancient Order of United Workmen and Mechanics, and V.A.S. (Vera Amicitia Sempiterna, "true friend-ship is eternal"). He set up the accounting systems and wrote the rituals for the latter two organizations.

No doubt, in his preparation of these and later rituals, he borrowed elements from Masonry, Odd Fellowship, and Pythianism....

Eventually, he would be responsible for the establishment of Modern Woodmen of America, Woodmen of the World Life Insurance Society, Woodmen of the World (Pacific Jurisdiction), Canadian Woodmen of the World, Supreme Forest Woodmen Circle, Neighbors of Woodcraft and, indirectly, Royal Neighbors of America.

In July 1882, Root heard a sermon by Rev. Sidney Crawford at First Congregational Church in Lyons, Iowa, about "pioneer woodmen clearing away the forest to provide for their families." Thus, he was inspired to organize Modern Woodmen of America as a society which would clear away problems of financial security for its members. He felt the use of the term "ancient" by so many fraternities was dishonest and, thus, described his order as "modern." He saw the word "woodmen" as alluding to a noble vocation. Since his order was native to American soil, he felt that the addition of the words "of America" was quite appropriate. He saw his brainchild as linked with his name of "Root" and visualized an order growing in the same manner as a tree in the forest grows from its roots.

On January 5, 1883, Root established Modern Woodmen of America at Lyons. He wrote the ritual and served as the first Venerable Consul of Pioneer Camp No. 1 and the first Head Consul of the new order. In 1888, the Royal Neighbors of America was established as a ladies auxiliary, with a relationship to the parent order similar to that of the Order of the Eastern Star to Masonry.[6]

With its history of connections with clandestine rituals, I have not been surprised when I have dealt with cases of demonic possession and curses that have come down from people whose direct ancestors were involved in Woodmen of the World. Because of those experiences, as well as what I have learned about the organization, I would not want to have an insurance policy with them under any circumstances, although I simply advise people who do carry a policy with them to follow their own conscience about cashing it out.

PROBLEMS WITH
CLANDESTINE ORGANIZATIONS

There are two key elements to the dangers of clandestine organizations: (1) the binding of one's heart and conscience to ungodly people and organizations, and (2) the actual swearing of oaths.

It is not that all clandestine organizations are positively Luciferian, but when people bind themselves together by soul ties, they open themselves to the ungodliness and evil of the others. When you have an organization whose members swear oaths in strictest secrecy, especially when those oaths involve injury and death as consequences, you have automatically created an environment in which curses and evil spirits can operate.

After His sermon on the mount, Jesus made His opinion clear on the subject of ungodly oaths:

> *Again you have heard that it was said to those of old, "You shall not swear falsely, but shall perform your oaths to the Lord." But I say to you, do not swear at all: neither by heaven, for it is God's throne; nor by the earth, for it is His footstool; nor by Jerusalem, for it is the city of the great King. Nor shall you swear by your head, because you cannot make one hair white or black. But let your "Yes" be "Yes," and your "No," "No." For whatever is more than these is from the evil one* (Matthew 5:33-37).

How much plainer could it be? No swearing of oaths is exempt. All clandestine cults evoke curses that are based on presumptive oaths. A presumptive oath is promising to do something that you do not have the power to perform, or that God forbids you to perform, such as murder or offering oneself to be killed. Far from being merely symbolic or illustrative, such oaths bring real curses with them. Jesus speaks His imperative words to all of His followers. Any time people cannot settle for a simple yes or no, but instead must underline their statements with oaths, they choose to submit themselves to someone or something other than Him.

The bottom line is this: Any organization—whether it calls itself a fraternity or a social service or even a church—is evil if it requires its members to commit themselves to each other and to the organization by means of secret vows, oaths, rituals, or ceremonies. This is especially true when those words of commitment would require members under some circumstances to perform immoral or illegal or life-threatening acts. Membership in such an organization is membership in a clandestine cult, and it brings an evil curse with it.

Not only should Christians not consider joining such an organization in the first place, but they also should examine their lives for evidence of curses that derive from the committed membership of past family members.

Breaking the demonic bondage of clandestine cults is vital for complete freedom. Life itself may depend on it.

ENDNOTES

1. For more information about these changes, see an article from *The Salt Lake City Messenger,* no. 75 (July 1990), by Jerald and Sandra Tanner, as posted on a Finnish website called "About Finnish Mormonism" accessed October 16, 2012 at www.mormonismi.net/temppeli/temple_ritual_altered4_utlm.shtml.

2. See *The Doctrine and Covenants,* posted online within the "Scriptures" section of the website, "The Church of Jesus Christ of Latter-Day Saints, accessed October 16, 2012, www.lds.org/scriptures/dc-testament/dc/129?lang=eng.

3. "The 11 O'clock toast," as posted on the website of the Elks, U.S.A., accessed October 16, 2012, www.elks.org/SharedElksOrg/lodges/files/1714_Eleven_o'clock_toast_01-17-2008.pdf. Also see the same post for more historical information.

4. Ibid.

5. "Woodmen of the World Burials," as posted on the website, accessed October 16, 2012, www.interment.net/wow/index.htm.

6. Robert L. Uzzel, "Joseph Cullen Root, 33°" on *SRJ Archives* (archives *of the Scottish Rite Journal*, Scottish Rite Freemasonry), accessed October 16, 2012, http://srjarchives.tripod.com/1998-09/UZZEL .HTM.

Chapter 7

UNEXPECTED CURSES

In the course of my ministry, scenes similar to this have been replayed hundreds of times. I start out by asking a person what hurt him or her the most in the past, and I get a response that's something like this one (from a middle-aged man):

"Rejection from my mother when I was in her womb, molestation by my uncle when I was seven, torment by other kids when I was in school. Something came over me. I just wanted to be suicidal. Now I am tormented by dreams of..." Already we can start to suspect that a demonic curse is involved.

In many of these cases, as with this man, the current evidence includes tormenting dreams, depression, and a persistent fear of acting out of perverted thought patterns. Meantime, he had been a Christian for quite some time.

He wants to be free. He remembers the facts of what happened to him as a child, but his memories are not clear—the pain, the fear, and the anger would be too much to handle. Now that we are about to break the curse of sexual abuse and get rid of the unclean spirit, I want him to detest what happened and to despise the enemy for what he did, so I command the demon, "Let him feel it when he was molested, the pain, the fear of it."

Don't touch me! Don't touch me! The man experiences what psychologists call an "abreaction." His emotions shift back to the time when he was violated, and he experiences the terror of that moment, as if it were happening in the now.

It is time now to confront the evil spirit that set up the sexual abuse.

"Come to attention and face me, you foul spirit."

He's a...

"He's what?"

He's a pervert!

"You have just cursed the property of God. This man belongs to Christ. He's covered in the blood of Christ. He's not a pervert."

I made him a pervert.

"No you haven't. Has he molested a child?"

No, but...

"Well then, he's not a pervert because you haven't got him to do it. You tried, but you failed. The best you could do was those filthy dreams."

The evil spirit, still speaking through the man's mouth and gestures, objects derisively, He had to get saved! That's all he thinks about. He's destroying our kingdom. He'll probably end up helping you.

Time to end this interrogation. I make the demon repeat after me: "Say, 'I, Perversion...'"

I, Perversion...

"...with all my kind..."

...with all my kind...

"...have no more right..."

(Speaking with difficulty) ...have no more right...

"We have no more right. We all receive..."

We all receive...

"...the judgment..."

Yeow!...the judgment...

"...of Almighty God."

...of Almighty God.

After further ministering of emotional healing to the man, it becomes plain that the evil spirit's hold is broken and the judgment of God is indeed being executed. I proceed to cast out the demon, much as I have described in other examples of this book. During an exorcism, there may be many unique aspects which are peculiar to that deliverance. But at the conclusion of the process, I usually stick closely to the protocol already detailed earlier, commanding the demonic intruder to announce its own doom and to declare that it acknowledges the judgment of tormenting consignment to the Abyss, the Pit. By having the demon declare its own expulsion, it is legally bound by the words it has spoken, "With all my kind, I go now to the Pit."

Once the demon has left the man who was tormented by thoughts of perversion, I anoint him with oil. "I declare that you are filled with the peace of God, the presence of Christ, and the comfort of the Holy Spirit. May the Lord take away the dreams, the nightmares, all the evil thoughts that were planted. We ask for the healing of his mind right now in Jesus' name."

"Praise God," the man testifies, with his wife by his side. "I just love the Lord. I want to serve Him with my whole life. Life is meaningless without Him. Just nothing, like Solomon said. Everything is meaningless except serving the Lord."

IS IT A CURSE?

Someone like this gentleman is a perfect example of how curses that have attached themselves to some event in the past can account for the private hell that the person has lived in. This man's dreams tormented him. He had to resist pedophiliac temptations all the time, and he lived in perpetual fear that he would abuse his own child or someone else's child the way he had been abused. He loved the Lord, and on his own would never abuse a child. Where were these thoughts coming from? What in the world was going on?

When he finally got the truth of what had happened out in the open in a safe place, he could be set free from the curse that had robbed him of so much. Satan seeks to wreak havoc on the human race by means of thousands of different kinds of curses, and some of them are easier to discern than others. Curses that come from cultic and occultic sources are fairly obvious. Others may masquerade as psychological damage or "bad luck" because the person carrying the curse bears emotional scars and struggles with circumstances of life.

Of course, not everything is a curse. Some things just happen in the course of normal life. Some bad choices produce worse fruit than others. But it is good to be able to recognize a potential curse, so you can deal with it effectively. Whenever someone is dealing with an intractable and distressing pattern of thoughts, behavior, or circumstances, you need to suspect a curse in addition to demonic infiltration. And much of the time, such curses have come from unsuspected sources in the past.

CURSES FROM UNEXPECTED SOURCES

By now, you should be familiar with the fact that curses can follow closely after overt sinful behavior, often behavior that occurred generations ago, and that the effect of a curse rises and falls depending on the godliness of the individuals it touches. Therefore, some of the following types of curses should not surprise you, although you may not have realized that certain problems could have arisen from such a thing as a curse. Some of the other ones may startle you and even upset you.

I am describing what I have discovered in the course of my own ministry spanning more than three decades. My hope is that this information will prove helpful to my readers, although each of you will have to decide prayerfully how to use it. I have broken the following curses often on behalf of Christians in North America and in more than a hundred nations worldwide.

The curse of slavery: The curse of slavery falls primarily on African Americans, but it also falls on those whose ancestors were white slave masters. Among African Americans, it manifests itself in an attitude of servitude and/or a continual hatred of white people, the idea that combative behavior against whites is the only way to get ahead in life. I see this curse at work when I see the contentiousness of certain well-known black agitators. (I do not see it in US President Barack Obama, to his credit. He's not stuck in that mindset, and that is probably one of the reasons he's been so successful in life.)

Among white people, the curse shows up as racism and false pride. Their ancestors acquired the curse of slavery when they demeaned their black-skinned slaves, and the current generation has perpetuated the attitude of superiority by virtue of mere skin color. Almost always when I work with either African Americans or white people who do not like black people, I take them through racial reconciliation to break these curses. This doesn't mean that either blacks or whites, or any other ethnic identity, is cursed per se as a race. It means that some individuals in such racial classifications may find it difficult to live in harmony with those historically perceived to be their subjects or their oppressors.

The curse of divorce: How many times have you said something like this? "Divorce just seems to run in that family." You may even see it in your own situation. To define it as a curse, it must be a strong pattern, not just an occasional divorce. In a family line with a curse of divorce, nobody seems to be able to make marriage work. Everybody gets divorced, parents and children, aunts, uncles, cousins, nieces, nephews, most of them more than once. This is not to say that divorced people as individuals are cursed simply because they failed in a marriage. But a curse of divorce in the bloodline may make it difficult to find and maintain stable marital relationships.

The curse of infertility: Not all infertility is the result of a curse, because it may result from a persistent and systemic physiological condition. But chronic barrenness in the family line, falling on some descendants (obviously not all or there would be no bloodline) can be a clue that a curse has been activated. In the Old Testament, infertility was often seen as a curse for some ancestral evil. The psalmist found it important to declare of the Lord, "He maketh the barren woman to keep house, and to be a joyful mother of children" (Ps. 113:9 KJV).

The curse of abandonment: I most often find this curse latching onto people who were given up for adoption or people who were young when their parents got divorced. When parents or custodians go in different directions, for whatever reason, children can feel rejected, and the curse of abandonment can come upon them. When a parent is gone incessantly due to work or other obligations, or when a parent fails to bond emotionally with a young child, this seeming neglect may inculcate in the offspring feelings of abandonment (if positive steps to affirm affection and significance are not deliberately taken). Satan will seize on such a situation to over-magnify the perceived abandonment in the mind of the child and to instill bitterness or a sense of worthlessness, both of which provide openings for a demonic curse.

The curse of sexual abuse: This was the curse that was broken in the story at the beginning of this chapter. You should suspect that this curse is operative whenever aberrant sexual behavior has been visited on a person. In cases of child molestation, rape, and incest, the aberration may duplicate itself in family members. In my extensive counseling experience I find that the majority of victims of sexual violation are demonically oppressed to some extent, and this victim's role somehow passes on to their children, who are often singularly at risk.

The curse of being badly born: The term "badly born" covers any kind of birth trauma. I sometimes ask people what they know about the circumstances of their birth, and I have heard some very interesting stories about what their mothers went through to give birth to them. Sometimes, of course, a difficult birth can be itself the result of a curse. Again, I am not saying that every difficult birth is the result of a curse. But such a curse can affect the mother adversely, causing emotional and even physical conditions that lead to a traumatic delivery. Sometimes the circumstances of birth terrorize the new infant so badly that he or she ends up seeing the world through the lens of a curse, and every environment seems to be a perpetually frightening place.

The curse of victimization: This is the curse that makes a person say, "I am always going to be abused and misused by someone else. Woe is me. I'll never get ahead in life. I am just a victim." This is a curse of never being able to rise above your circumstances because some part of you believes that it is your lot in life to get the short end of the stick.

This curse may be rooted in ancestors who were persecuted or suffered some form of disenfranchisement. I sometimes find it in those who have Jewish ancestry, especially those who relatives suffered the Holocaust. In Eastern Europe, it is experienced by people whose parents lived under the totalitarianism of Soviet Russia. African Americans, Native Americans, and First Nations peoples also can have this curse because they are the descendants of slavery and genocide. Those whose ancestors were sexually violated generation after generation may unconsciously be at risk because they act in a vulnerable rather than a confident manner. This curse is broken by declaring that in Christ we are a new creation (see 2 Corinthians 5:17) and become victors instead of victims.

The curse of procrastination: This curse...well, never mind. Maybe I just don't feel like telling you about it. Here's what I'll do; I will put it in my next book....

Seriously, there is such a thing as a curse of procrastination—although not every incidence of procrastination comes from a curse. Far from it! You can begin to suspect a curse if you notice a definite pattern of procrastination in a family. Some people raise procrastination to an art form. I have wondered if whole nationalities are plagued with this curse.

Putting off the inevitable or important, when it is not merely a bad behavioral trait, can be spiritually disenabling. It makes people avoid critical decisions and life challenges. I see it in those who marry late, hold on to damaging relationships, put off educational pursuits, fail to care for personal health or weight issues, and delay spiritual goals such as Bible reading. These individuals are always looking for the "right church," while attending none, and they fret over having the wrong job, while never writing a new resume.

Let's be clear. All these characteristics may be the result of human conditions and have nothing to do with the supernatural. The difference is whether or not a person's bloodline shows such crippling conduct as part of a pattern. It could go back to some ancestor's decision to avoid emotional pain or refusal to accept some important spiritual choice, thus hampering future generations with a dread of decision making.

The curse of isolation: I call this malady the curse of being stuck in Jerusalem. You know, the curse that limits people from getting out and doing things to fulfill their calling and purpose. They never "get out of Jerusalem" to Judea and Samaria and the uttermost parts of the earth (see Acts 1:8).

How does this look? A person stuck in isolation finds it difficult to accept challenges in relationships. People may be single because of this, never extending themselves emotionally to others. They live under a kind of a lockdown. They do not want to become vulnerable, so they never reach out. Others may be stuck in a dead-end job or a vocation they detest. They could decide to get out of it, but they don't do it. They are stuck in Jerusalem.

Do not misunderstand me; as with all of these curses, not every lonely person is afflicted with the curse of isolation nor is every unhappy worker under a curse. But I consistently encounter evil spirits who go by the name Isolation. Their job it is to keep their host separated from human contact, outside the community of fellow worshippers of Christ, and mired in loneliness. In extreme cases, the victim suffers from agoraphobia, never leaving the house except occasionally for necessities.

"I want this person for myself so I can control them," the demons of this curse tell me. To break this curse I encourage isolated people to develop an accountability group, at least a small circle of friends who can monitor their behavior on a regular basis. The demonic intent of this curse is to get the isolated individual to recycle thoughts and emotions without external, objective input. Friends are the means whereby we test our ideas and expose our issues in a safe context. Without that, the isolated victim may hear only the inner voices of demons or the suggestions of the devil.

This curse can come from a smothering parent who wants to keep a child forever to herself or himself. No potential mate is ever good enough to win the approval of Mom or Dad. I have encountered cases of a health-challenged parent who was determined to keep a child as a readily available caregiver and, therefore, has denigrated every relationship the adult child tried to develop. It may not seem like an evil trap to have Mom in the nursing home, demanding your constant communication, which hinders your social development, but demons will exploit even the best of intentions to keep you in the curse of isolation.

This curse is also complicated by ancestors who withdrew to a state of separateness because of fear or persecution. They may have been persecuted for religious or ethnic reasons to the point that it seemed to be safer to avoid outside contact. Physical and sexual abuse also plays into this pattern. If one's parents or grandparents, for example, were violated, they may have found it easier to retreat to an inner emotional state and try to avoid further abuse by appearing to be "invisible." The template is then established to withdraw in every area of life so as to obtain a false sense of safety.

God has created us for community, and we are all healthier in every way when we are connected to the larger human family, especially our brothers and sisters in Christ. That's why the Bible says that serious decisions in life should have the checks and balances described in Proverbs 11:14: "Where there is no counsel, the people fall; but in the multitude of counselors there is safety." To break the curse of isolation, the segregated person must take the initiative to reach out to whatever friendships and alliances are available and build upon them. The hold of the devil will gradually disperse, and the demons will no longer have that person to themselves.

Curses associated with blood transfusions and organ transplants: Sometimes people ask me about the possibility of inheriting a curse from an unrelated person by means of a blood transfusion or an organ transplant. The Bible does not explicitly prohibit blood transfusions or organ transplants, because such things were impossible to medical science when the Bible was written. Scripture does say that "the blood is the life" (Deut. 12:23).

We know that the blood of another person would always accompany a donated transplant organ, and we know that curses are carried in the "bloodline." This fact is spiritual and metaphorical, but it can also be literal. I have dealt with cases of demonic possession in which the demon claimed a legal right through either a transfusion or an organ transplant. If the organ donor carried a generational curse in his or her genetic code, it could be "donated" along with the physical organ or blood.

Once when I was hospitalized, I received a blood transfusion. The order came at night when I was alone. I immediately called my wife so we could agree together in prayer that the blood I was about to receive would have every curse broken from it. If I were to receive an organ transplant, I would pray in the same way. I would trust God to break every curse attached to the organ or blood so that I could gladly receive the organ, assured that the power of God's Word can shatter every curse.

CREMATION

Now I want to present some material that many people find controversial—the idea of a curse being attached to the act of cremation. I want to explain to you why I think this is true.

Throughout history, it has been the pagans, the followers of demonic and occult religions, who have cremated their dead. They build their funeral pyres and watch their loved ones' bodies burn to ashes without anguish, because many of them believe that the body is evil, while the spirit is pure, and that for the body to release the soul into its next stage of reincarnation in the next life, it cannot remain encased in the evil, decaying body. The survivors do not expect to see their loved ones again.

Christians and Jews, however, believe that the soul and spirit are already released to God at the moment of death. As a statement of faith, in opposition to the beliefs of the Greco-Roman world in which they lived, the early church buried its dead. That's why the subterranean catacombs in Rome are lined with graves. In death as it was in life, the body receives honor. Christians and Jews have always laid dead bodies to rest in the way that they were known in life.

In North America, cremation was almost unheard-of as recently as 1900. By 1972, the frequency of cremation had risen to about 5 percent, and by 20 years later, it was up to 20 percent as a preferred method of treating a person's body after death. As recently as 2010, 40 percent of Americans have been cremated after death, and of course the percentage is still increasing.

As a disposition of choice, cremation is much more economical than traditional burial, and it provides much more flexibility in terms of memorial services. Nobody should feel guilty if they have made a decision to have the body of a loved one cremated or if they have written cremation into their own final wishes. But we should recognize the fact that cremation removes a significant amount of "closure" from the process of death.

The three-hour cremation process erases the memorial of the body that will be raised from the dead someday. The crematorium operator scrapes the granules and fragments into a cardboard box the size of a shoe box, which can be buried, scattered, shipped, or allowed to collect dust on the mantel. Cremation fits our fast-food mentality. We do not have a wake. We do not want to feel. We do not want to grieve or think about life after death.

The ancient Jews, followed by the early Christians and the Muslims, found cremation unthinkable. In fact, if they could not properly care for a body before burial, they at least wanted the bones to be buried with care. Joseph wanted his bones brought back from Egypt. (See Genesis 50:25; Exodus 13:19.) When Saul committed suicide and the enemies of Israel took his body and staked it up against the wall, the faithful people of Israel came and collected his bones to make sure that they would be buried. (See 2 Samuel 21:12-14. It is true that they burned the body first, but that was for practical hygienic reasons as well as for reasonable transportation considerations.)

For practical or civil reasons, cremation may be the best option at times, for example, if a person is living in a country where space is at a premium and everyone who dies must be cremated. In times of war or natural disaster or plague, cremation may be the only way to prevent the spread of disease. But when the option of Christian burial is available, why choose the unbiblical method? Why court the opportunity to acquire a curse by "doing as the pagans do"?

Paul summarized the biblical approach to death and burial in chapter 15 of his letter to the church at Corinth, which I commend to your reading. Now you can read it with fresh understanding:

> *For I delivered to you first of all that which I also received: that Christ died for our sins according to the Scriptures, and that He was buried, and that He rose again the third day according to the Scriptures, and that He was seen by Cephas, then by the twelve....*
>
> *Now if Christ is preached that He has been raised from the dead, how do some among you say that there is no resurrection*

of the dead? But if there is no resurrection of the dead, then Christ is not risen. And if Christ is not risen, then our preaching is empty and your faith is also empty. Yes, and we are found false witnesses of God, because we have testified of God that He raised up Christ, whom He did not raise up—if in fact the dead do not rise. For if the dead do not rise, then Christ is not risen. And if Christ is not risen, your faith is futile; you are still in your sins! Then also those who have fallen asleep in Christ have perished. If in this life only we have hope in Christ, we are of all men the most pitiable (1 Corinthians 15:3-5, 12-19).

TATTOOS AND BODY PIERCINGS

You would not know it by looking at the people in a public place on a hot summer day, but the people of God have some biblical catching up to do when it comes to tattoos and body piercing. We can start by reading God's command to the people of Israel: "You shall not make any cuttings in your flesh for the dead, nor tattoo any marks on you: I am the Lord" (Lev. 19:28).

It is one thing for non-Christians to get tattoos. Non-Christians make lots of decisions that bear no reference to God's desires. If such people subsequently become Christians, they continue to carry the bodily evidence of their former lives before becoming new in Christ. That evidence can be borne in other ways, too, and I do not want to send anybody on a guilt trip.

It is another matter when a Christian who knows the Word of God decides to get "inked." It is just not a spiritually smart thing to do, and the same goes for the self-mutilation that goes with body piercings. Granted, not many piercings are undertaken on behalf of the dead as the passage above prohibits, but other Old Testament passages deplore the practice of drawing blood by slicing one's own skin, and they link it with demonic worship. (See, for example, First Kings 18:28 about the prophets of Baal on Mt. Carmel and Mark 5:5 about the Gadarene demoniac.)

Because both tattooing and body piercing involve piercing the skin and because such skin piercing has primitive spiritual associations, tattooing and body piercing can (and do) give openings to demonic curses. I have encountered situations in which I could not get demons to leave people until they took out their body piercings. One time a woman had a piercing in her navel which was hidden from my sight by her clothing. The demons simply would not obey when I tried to cast them out. I persisted and forced the evil spirits to reveal their source of strength. (Think about it. The navel represents the prenatal, bodily source of life.)

It was the stud in her navel that they were attached to and that had given them permission to enter her life. So I had some ladies who were assisting me in ministry take her aside, and she pulled up her blouse so they could take out the stud. The demons left immediately. Experiences like that one are revealing in more ways than one.

In another case, a woman tormented by demons resisted all attempts to receive deliverance. She happened to lean over momentarily to tie her sneaker, exposing the lower part of her back, where she had a so-called "tramp stamp" tattoo at the base of her spine. When she sat upright again, I asked her permission to simply place my Bible over that spot. She leaned forward, and I had a lady ministering with me put the Bible directly over the tattoo. The woman instantly screamed in a full-blown demonic manifestation and flew off the couch, writhing on the floor in demonic convulsions.

The base of the spine is a particularly popular spot for tattoos. Because this location on the human body coincides with the muladhara chakra (a psychic center) of Hinduism, it is used to awaken the kundalini, or power of the serpent, in yoga. Since they are intended to enhance spiritual enlightenment in union with God, spiritual curses can fall on those who obtain such tattoos.

In yet another case, a Christian mother brought to me her teenage daughter who was experiencing a strange eye disorder that caused occasional, temporary blindness and piercing headaches. I realized that if this physical attack were demonic the only way that Satan could attack the daughter was through the mother, unless the child was involved in some sin or occult indulgence. I spoke with the daughter extensively and eliminated all possible explanations for a demonic opening through her own misconduct. Meantime, the mother sat in a chair opposite me with her legs crossed, wearing summer shorts that came to just below her knee. My eyes were drawn to something I had not noticed before. On the calf of her leg was a large tattoo of a wolf. I asked why the tattoo, and she told me that the she'd had a fascination with wolves since she was a child.

"May I take the cross I use when ministering deliverance and touch that tattoo?" I asked.

"Sure."

I didn't just touch it. I directed the pointed apex of the cross at the tattoo and made a stabbing motion as if spiritual piercing the wolf. Demons instantly came to attention and lunged toward me to pull back the cross, screaming, "Stop! How did you know our power was in that tattoo?"

It turned out that the one needing ministry was the mother. She was the one carrying the curse, which had passed on to physically torment her child. Through the exorcism process, we eventually uncovered a curse going back nearly a thousand years to Nordic ancestors who worshiped the god Loki, whose son Fenrir is portrayed as a wolf. We anointed the tattoo with oil, canceled the curse it represented, and proceeded with the deliverance process of freeing both mother and child.

Both tattoos and body piercing are associated with pagan cultures. The word tattoo comes from a Tahitian word tatu, and the practice was reintroduced to the Western world in the 1700s by sailors who had visited the Polynesian islands. I say "reintroduced" because before Europe was Christianized, tattoos were common, as they still are in countless non-Christian cultures. In Western Europe and North America, tattoos remained largely the province of sailors and soldiers for the past couple of centuries, until not long ago.

For most of the history of tattoos and other body-defacing practices, people believed that the marks carried some kind of power. Tattoos and scarification (achieved by rubbing a pigment into a cut or by irritating the cut so that it leaves a noticeable scar) identify people as members of particular cultural groups. They helped their bearers gain access to the spirit world or they served as a rite-of-passage fertility talisman for young men and women entering adulthood. Special tattoos were inked to encourage healing and to draw down magical powers. In some cases, such as in Hindu self-mutilation ceremonies, hanging and pulling by the flesh is part of devotion to pagan gods. Then too, tattoos were also used up until modern times to designate prisoners and criminals; think of the numbers forcibly tattooed on the forearms of prisoners in Nazi concentration camps.

Can we really relate these practices to the modern fad of inking some design into the skin or piercing almost any part of the body that is pierceable? I would exempt from this ear piercing for the purpose of wearing earrings. In thousands of documented case studies of exorcism, I have never encountered a curse or instance of demonic possession related to pierced earlobes. I have, however, faced countless cases of satanic legal rights of entry claimed through metal inserted in tongues, navels, lips, and so forth. To be honest, it is difficult to call beautiful a circular pendant hanging from the pierced septum of a woman's nose.

Also, we need to be reasonable about body art that might cover unsightly birthmarks (so long as the tattoo isn't something demonic such as a dragon) or tattoos that help to fade out a birthmark. I see nothing against tattoos that are used as medical identifiers or to enhance breast reconstruction after surgery. I also leave open to the reader his or her own conclusions about tattoos that depict Scriptures or biblical themes. They certainly are not a spiritual hindrance on the same level as the "ink art" of a voluptuous woman or a serpent. In my opinion, however, any physical defacement potentially providing demonic facilitation is too great a risk to consider.

Here are several reasons that I object to certain forms of ornamental tattooing or body piercing:

1. Consulting a tattooist is tantamount to consulting a witch doctor, given the long and colorful (pardon the pun) history of the art. Like the witch doctor, the tattooist is marking the body for some purpose that usually is anti-biblical, such as tattoos of demonic beings or symbols

of the non-Christian world (pentacles, pentagrams, erotic images, snakes, dragons, Buddhist mandalas, mythological gods, obscene words, representations of soul-tie relationships, satanic slogans such as "Born to Be Wild" or "Live to Die," and so forth).

2. In some cases, the tattoo is the actual embodiment of the demon. As I have already pointed out, one of the most popular creatures depicted in tattoos is the dragon. It is not just because dragons are popular in Eastern cultures. It is because, as the Bible says, the devil is a "dragon" (see Revelation 20:2). Satan wants his symbol on you to mark his ownership.

3. Pagan societies believe that *mana*, the spiritual force of the soul as defined in Pacific Island cultures, is manifested, and thus indwelt, by a tattoo. This *mana* (similar to *chi* in oriental cultures and *prana* in Hinduism) represents the pagan, primordial essence of spiritual power that is believed to flow through and animate all living things, the "life-force" counterpart to the Christian belief in the *logos*, identified as Christ, the creator of all life. The tattoo is a stamp recognizing this *mana*. That is not to say that a Westerner is conceding to this philosophy by merely getting a tattoo, but the tattooed person has no way of knowing if his ancestors may have practiced such false religions. By having the tattoo, there may be a demonic link to this past evil.

4. The simple injection of ink under the skin has no spiritual power within itself. Neither does the ink-imprinted cardboard of an Ouija board. It is the particular subject, theme, art, saying, or representation that causes the damage. Symbols have the power to bridge the gap between the physical and the metaphysical, the visible and the invisible world. Identifying with certain symbols

(a pentagram, for example) represents a regrettable contact with the spirit world.

5. Practically speaking, tattoos and body piercings can damage future job prospects and relationships. Some companies will not hire a person with an obvious tattoo or piercing. The interview process is too late to persuade them otherwise. And what if you have the name of your current girlfriend or boyfriend tattooed on your body, only to switch to someone else in due time? (Not to mention how that up-to-the-minute tattoo is going to look on 80-year-old skin someday.)

WHAT TO DO ABOUT CURSES FROM UNFORESEEN SOURCES

God has not left us without a solution to the damage of such unusual curses. John the Baptist, speaking of the Savior who was coming soon, said, "Even now the ax is laid to the root of the trees. Therefore every tree which does not bear good fruit is cut down and thrown into the fire" (Matt. 3:10). In other words, to prepare the way for the saving and life-changing power of God, we need to take a spiritual ax to the unhealthy roots (curses and more) that have made our lives bear bad fruit.

We need to confess our position, not our condition. When we are subject to one of these kinds of curses, we should not keep reinforcing the curse by repeating the details of our condition, acting out of the assumption that this is just the way things are meant to be. ("Woe is me. I was abandoned. I had a rough start in life. If things had been different, I wouldn't be this way. Nobody loves me or wants me or cares about me.") It is all right to acknowledge a less-than-perfect condition, but that's not where we want to stay. We need to confess our standing in Christ and the freedom that He brings, speaking out of a disciple's earnest desire to learn what that means by firsthand experience. God will meet us and show us what to do.

Finally, we need to make the behavioral changes that are necessary for full freedom. It is one thing to identify a curse and renounce it, even to speak words of renunciation about certain actions and attitudes, but it is another thing to walk away and make real lifestyle changes. We need to change our course. Most likely, the curse was able to land because we had bad behavior patterns to begin with. Then the curse reinforced the behavior, and it became more deeply rooted. Part of laying the ax to the root is getting rid of the bad root, so that bad fruit will not have a chance anymore. If good behavioral changes occur, the curse has no place to land. If the former environment gets changed for the better, the old curse will no longer be welcome.

This may involve some good counseling, inner healing, and godly therapy. Or it may be enough to take time for self-evaluation and intro-spection. Why was this curse so effective? What needs to change? What will it take to make those changes happen, and how can we make sure that the changes stick?

None of us wants to stay stuck in a dead-end curse. God doesn't want us to stay stuck, either. He has a destiny and a plan for every life, and the more completely we break free from old curses, the sooner we can get on with a life of freedom and joy.

Chapter 8

TAKING ACTION AGAINST SATAN TO BREAK CURSES

Sometimes you can stop a curse before it lands on you. That's what I did once after a seminar, when a lady walked up to me. She was nicely dressed and soft-spoken. "Pastor Larson," she said, "I'd like to pray with you, and I have some things I'd like to share with you."

"Well, that's wonderful," I replied.

She reached out and put her hand on my shoulder and began to pray: "Lord Jesus, I thank you for this wonderful man of God. I thank you for what he means to me and what a blessing he is in my life. Thank you, Jesus, for anointing him to help me in so many ways. And Lord Jesus, I ask you to please show this dear man of God the error of his ways, where he's gone wrong, the false teaching that he's giving…"

I interrupted her. "Stop it."

"Excuse me?" She opened her eyes wide in reaction to my blunt, unexpected response.

I said it again: "Stop! Be quiet."

"Well," she sputtered, "I am praying for you!"

"No, you're not," I replied. "You're cursing me."

"What!?" The woman backed up a couple of steps.

I repeated, "You're cursing me. I want you to stop it and be quiet."

She put her hands on her hips and faced me. "Well, I thought you were a man of God, and I just wanted to bless you and pray over you."

I contradicted her, "No, you didn't. You're trying to curse me. You're speaking evil over my life and accusing me of heresy. I do not give you the right to do that. Stop it, now."

She lifted her hands as if she wanted to lay them on me again. "I always thought you were so spiritual. And the Lord gave me a word for you. I was just about to share it."

"I don't care. Be quiet and get out of here." I knew it sounded rude, but it seemed like the only way I could get her to leave.

She turned around and started to walk away, got halfway down the aisle, and turned around to have the last word: "F––– you, preacher."

Now I knew for sure where this woman was coming from. If you give Jezebel a little bit of time, she always gives herself away. I also knew that, too often, people come with loving-sounding words, and then they slowly start to twist the knife, changing their words into something else.

I had dodged a curse-ball. Not a bad way to end a seminar on curse breaking.

We all need to be very careful who speaks into our lives. Just because people claim to be prophets or they preface their words with "I say this in love," or "I don't want you to be hurt by what I'm about to say," that does not mean we have to receive their words passively. Far better to risk offending someone than to be saddled with an unexpected curse, even if it is a relatively minor one.

LAWSUIT AGAINST SATAN

It is vital for each of us to stand strong on our legal rights as people who have been redeemed by Jesus Christ. Not only will that help us to dodge curses in the course of our daily lives, but it can also help us get rid of curses we may have been carrying, as we become aware of them. Sometimes such curses have been newly activated, and other times they have been lurking in our family line for generations.

Several years ago, the Lord put into my mind the idea of bringing a lawsuit against the devil, of holding the enemy legally accountable, in a spiritual sense. I have refined it over time, and I take it very seriously.

When I present it for people to use, I want them to have the same sense of determination. This lawsuit is best "filed" when spoken aloud, preferably in the company of other Christians, and signed as indicated below. You may even choose to do it with a prayer group or with an entire congregation.

WRIT, COMPLAINT, AND JUDGMENT AGAINST SATAN AND HIS KINGDOM

In the name of Jesus Christ, I, _____, known as the plaintiff, approach the courts of Heaven and declare the following complaint on behalf of myself against the Enemy of my soul, now known as the defendant, Satan. In the name of Christ our Lord, I apply the blood of Jesus over this case and demand that proper judgment be executed forthwith by Christ, who has fully resolved this complaint by His sacrifice upon the cross. As the above-mentioned plaintiff I have the legal right to enforce this claim through the authority which Christ has given me. This action is now called the Judgment of God and is considered a total and complete vindication against all demonic actions against me and is executed by order of the one and true God, also known as the Messiah, the Prince of Peace, the Everlasting Father, the Great I Am, and all other names by which He, the Living God, is known.

I hereby file suit for the following complaints:

Complaint #1:

All direct and indirect actions against the plaintiff to hinder and affect the plaintiff's health or quality of life with any chronic, debilitating, or deadly condition, sickness, illness, or disease that has been caused, assigned, or been plotted against said plaintiff, and for any and all injuries and trauma, either physical, mental, spiritual, psychological, or emotional that have been directed toward the plaintiff.

Complaint #2:

All direct and indirect attacks upon any and all relationships of the plaintiff, including the plaintiff's family, loved ones, and all those with whom the plaintiff has relationships.

Complaint #3:

All direct and indirect curses, hexes, vexes, jinxes, satanic assignments, demonic oppression, and witchcraft rituals that may have been sent, or are being sent, or ever will be sent to the plaintiff, as well as any malicious actions, such as harassment, whether mental, physical, spiritual, or emotional.

All the above complaints are filed with the courts of Heaven and seven-fold restitution is demanded, along with all property that the enemy has stolen or has directly or indirectly caused to be harmed, injured, or assaulted. I now file this lawsuit and complaint in the high courts of Heaven against the enemy, the defendant, the one called Satan, the Prince of Darkness, the power of the air, Lucifer, the great Dragon, the Serpent of old, the accuser of the brethren, and all other names and entities known or unknown representing this adversary, whether he is or has been represented either in spirit or in person through any workers of darkness; this complaint includes their assignments through ceremonies, soul ties, dedications, blood curses, blood oaths, satanic ceremonies, or blood covenants. I also include in this suit all generational curses, works done by witches and Satanists, including but not limited to all the names used by all these representatives of the defendant, whether earthly or demonic.

Determination:

Collection and judgment of said lawsuit and complaint is now immediate without the possibility of appeal. This decision is declared final by the Judge of all humanity, One Father, One God, in three Persons, the Eternal Magistrate.

Judgments:

1. All goods, property, wealth, monies that have been stolen and taken from the plaintiff, directly or indirectly, are now to be returned and restored by the defendant seven times the actual value of the original goods taken from the above-named plaintiff.

2. All health is to be returned to the plaintiff and all attacks upon the plaintiff's present health are now broken, cut off, and severed by the blood of Jesus Christ. Restitution of health is to be seven times the original condition before such attacks occurred.

3. All those who by relationships have been negatively affected by and toward the plaintiff, including the plaintiff's family, loved ones, and all those associated with the plaintiff, are now to be freed from all oppressions, sickness, illness, disease, and torment. All relationships are to be restored to seven times their original value.

4. All curses, ill-spoken words, assignments, attacks, insults, hexes, vexes, jinxes, or any ungodly words uttered, directly or indirectly by the enemy against the plaintiff, are now nullified. If any of those parties or entities, known or unknown, will not cancel these uttered maledictions, then all these evil entities will be held accountable and liable to judgment rendered by the Eternal Magistrate.

By order of the Court of Heaven:

Judgment for the plaintiff, _____, is now ordered in the name of Christ Jesus the Lord and by the blood of the Lamb.

I, _____, the plaintiff have set my hand to affirm the same, this day of _____, the year of our Lord, 2_____ .

Signature of plaintiff

_____ _____

I/we, _____ _____ have agreed (see Matthew 18:19) with this complaint and have set my/our hand(s) as a witness this _____ day of _____, the year of our Lord, 2_____ .

The above is ratified in the most holy name of Jesus Christ the Lord, to whom all honor and glory and praise belong. Amen and forever Amen.

This lawsuit against the devil can be reviewed in whole or in part from time to time so that you can remember that you belong to Jesus Christ and what that means in terms of your freedom from the opposing kingdom of darkness.

TEN STEPS TO BREAK CURSES

Until they read the legal-sounding document above, most people do not know that they can bring a lawsuit against the devil and win. Because of Jesus's sacrifice on the cross, the power of His adversary has been shattered. It is only a matter of time before Lucifer himself will be sentenced to eternal banishment and impotence.

In the meantime, we need to position ourselves. We need not only to announce our legal rights, but also to renounce everything that has to do with the kingdom of darkness. Here is a quick review of what we have learned in this book in the form of the ten steps we can take to clear our lives of curses and their fallout:

1. *Confess Jesus Christ.* Curses can be broken only by the power of Jesus. No curse can be completely and totally removed from your life unless you know Jesus Christ as your personal Savior and Lord.

Curses can be partially alleviated by a change in behavior. Whether or not a person knows Christ, curses can be removed to some extent by a basic repudiation of evil. This is a positive development, of course. But curse breaking can never be finalized until a person confesses Jesus Christ as Lord.

On occasion, when I am working with people who are not Christians, I take the process of curse breaking and deliverance and healing as far as I can, and then I say something like, "OK, I have taken you as far as I can take you. Now you have to personally put your trust in Christ." Most of the time, they do, and we can finish what we started.

2. *Renounce the devil.* Satan and all that he represents must be directly repudiated. It is never enough to rest on the assumption that

someone who has just accepted the lordship of Jesus now wants nothing more to do with the devil. People must say so, out loud.

To move forward, people must not only take hold of Jesus's hand, but they must release the hand of the devil, who is holding them back. A yes to Jesus must be followed by a no to the devil. Throughout Church history, in baptisms, confirmations, and confessional professions of faith, a repudiation of the devil has always been included.

3. ***Renounce vows.*** Renouncing all vows (citing as many specifics as necessary and feasible) is part of basic curse breaking. I define a vow as a solemn promise by which a person has become bound to act in a certain way. Again, this is good to do out loud, even if nobody in particular is listening. It is more meaningful and intentional that way. Always try to have other Christians present as a witness to comply with the principle we've already stated in this book (see Matthew 18:19).

4. ***Renounce oaths.*** How do oaths differ from vows? My definition of an oath is, "a solemn confirmation of the consequences of keeping or breaking a vow." When a man promises to uphold the secrets of membership in a Masonic lodge, as pointed out earlier, he adds this oath:

> ...binding myself under no less penalty than to have my left breast torn open and my heart and vitals taken from thence and thrown over my left shoulder and carried into the valley of Jehoshaphat, there to become a prey to the wild beasts of the field, and vulture of the air, if ever I should prove willfully guilty of violating any part of this my solemn oath or obligation of a Fellow Craft Mason; so help me God....

The Masonic vow swears allegiance to the group. The words of the oath represent the binding enforcement of the vow. This book has mentioned a variety of oaths that bring curses. We need to make sure to include as many of them as we can catalogue.

5. ***Renounce rituals.*** Vows and oaths are often made in the context of rituals, which can be defined as a prescribed format of words and actions governing an act of worship or spiritual obedience. Rituals need to be renounced, too, along with the intention behind the words and

actions. Rituals involve a certain sequence of motions and set of proceedings, sometimes with chanting, hocus-pocus, incantation, or other verbal confirmation. When a curse has sprung from participation in a ritual (even when that ritual was undertaken in the past by a distant ancestor), then the ritual itself, which was the starting place of the curse, must be renounced.

6. *Renounce ceremonies.* Rituals take place in the context of ceremonies; they are specific routines within a larger formal procedure. Rituals reinforce the ceremony. For example, a ceremony of blood covenant may involve certain rituals such as drinking blood, desecrating a cross or a Bible, or incantations to specific deities. This entwines the ceremony into the root structure of the curse, and in order to pull out the curse entirely, the entire ceremony must be repudiated.

7. *Renounce blood covenants.* Blood covenants are rare in the modern world. But in the world of the ancients, they were very widespread. We know they were common in Africa, and we see abundant evidence for them in the Old Testament in the polytheistic heathen people groups.

Blood covenants are oaths sealed with blood, sometimes animal blood, sometimes human. They most often require the death of the animal or person (often a child), which is much more serious than ordinary bloodletting.

When breaking modern-day curses, often we need to break off ancient curses that stem from blood covenants. It is important to know whether a covenant involved animal blood, human blood, or both. Stronger, more enforceable, curses result from human blood sacrifices.

8. *Renounce witchcraft and sorcery.* Witchcraft and sorcery forge alliances with evil spirits, who are called upon through divination for increased power and dominance. In order to break all curses, a person must renounce any connections with witchcraft and sorcery, including distant family connections.

We must remember also the words spoken to King Saul after he disobeyed God's clear command: "For rebellion is as the sin of witchcraft, and stubbornness is as iniquity and idolatry. Because you have rejected the word of the Lord, He also has rejected you from being king" (1 Sam. 15:23). Comprehensive curse breaking includes a renunciation of rebellion against God's commandments.

9. ***Renounce false gods.*** Along with renouncing the mode of approach to gain increased power through spiritual access, we must renounce the false gods themselves. We must deny every obligation to every demon of false worship. Sometimes it will be necessary, when possible, to mention specific demonic deities by name. Even if we ourselves have not worshipped false gods, our ancestors may have made sacrifices or dedicated themselves to unseen evil powers. Demonic possession often occurs by the evil spirit taking the name and function of some ancient divinity, such as Isis or Horus, Ashtoreth or Moloch. Through obeisance, our ancestors may have forged powerful soul-tie relationships with these gods which continue unbroken to this day. By breaking that attachment now, it removes the legal right claimed by the demon who is named after a particular false god.

10. ***Renounce false religions.*** To wrap it up, we must renounce and denounce every cult or religious system in which we ourselves or our ancestral line has become entangled. Any religious system that stands in opposition to Christ (including a few that name His name, while not representing His truth) must be repudiated, and we must reaffirm our allegiance to the Lord Jesus Christ Himself.

These ten steps reflect the two basic elements necessary for breaking any curse: Say it and Believe it. Just as it is with salvation, we must confess what we believe—and really believe what we confess.

Remember the words of Romans 10:9-10:

> *If you confess with your mouth, "Jesus is Lord," and believe in your heart that God raised him from the dead, you will be saved. For it is with your heart that you believe and are justified, and it is with your mouth that you confess and are saved* (NIV).

Everyone who enters the Kingdom of God does so by means of a confession of faith—saying what they believe. You announce your new intention to obey God and accept Jesus Christ as your Savior, you renounce your sins and former intentions, and you confirm the words of your declaration in your heart. Announce, renounce, ratify. Say it and believe it. The same principle that holds true for salvation is applicable to breaking away from the kingdom of darkness.

Some people will do this instinctively, but most of us need to be taught. It is not good enough to act compliant on the surface while remaining a rebel at heart. Demons have sometimes taunted me with statements such as, "Yeah, he's saying the words, but he doesn't believe it." Such words can be just a demonic bluff, but not always. The demons know when a person is just going through the motions, trying to satisfy the process. If people do not really mean what they declare, nothing will change.

Both salvation and curse breaking take place on two levels. First is the natural level of articulating certain words. Second, and even more important, is the spiritual dimension—what is inside the person's heart. What a person believes in the heart makes all the difference.

PROGRESSIVE VICTORY

Complete curse breaking is within our reach, but it does not happen in one easy session. In His mercy, God knows that we can take only so much change at one time and that full freedom comes by degrees. As we shed one curse and the demons that accompany it, following through with new behaviors and expectations, He can give us a better perspective from which to see additional patterns that need attention. It is a progressive victory.

I was working with one man, and even after more than two dozen sessions, we had not cleared out all of the undergrowth of curses. He was fully cooperative, but each session wiped him out so thoroughly that we had to adjourn until another time. His progress was very real but so were the curses that we were demolishing.

Here is a taste of what we did together: We started out in our first session dealing with a spirit of Witchcraft, a seven-generation curse of Jezebel, Incest, Poverty, and Infirmity. Then in the second session, we dealt with the spirit of Death, another spirit of Witchcraft, and evil deities associated with various historical false religious systems, including ancient Babylon, Assyria, and Egypt, to name a few. Curses attached to each of these evil kingdoms had to be renounced.

At our third session, we concentrated on spirits of Isolation and Mind Control, breaking more curses along the way. Subsequent sessions led us to eliminate the influence of several more arcane Babylonian gods, Egyptian deities, and spirits of Illuminati. We also dealt with very antagonistic anti-Christ spirits of Deception and Death going back 34 generations to Irish ancestors. We confronted the Scandinavian pagan gods named Thor and Odin. We reversed and unwound rituals and oaths. We broke ties to gods and goddesses, some of which even I had never heard of. We never knew what was coming next.

Working back and forth chronologically as things came up, we plundered the kingdoms of darkness and freed this man from spirits of Insanity, Failure, Bondage, Fear, and Torment. I am giving you only a quick summary of this spiritual saga that played out over many months. The man was in no way impeding our prayers or efforts. It is just that his family line had been so ravaged by evil that it took a very long time and many hours of curse breaking to methodically work through and eradicate every evidence of the works of darkness.

This experience is worth bearing in mind as you take a God-assisted look at patterns in your own life. While curse breaking is essentially a done deal once you understand the basics, it is almost never as simple as "out, in the name of Jesus." Each one of us must be committed to a systematic, methodical approach as we continue to work over issues that come to the surface. It takes time. Your life in the meantime gets better with each victory, and God can use you mightily even while you remain a "work in progress."

As God gives you the grace and the opportunity, and as He brings greater revelation about your situation, He will bring you to another level of freedom. Even if you have already gone through basic curse-breaking prayers and renunciations, such as what you will find in the final section of this book, it never hurts to go through it again. You never know when you might snag something you missed before.

The more you learn about curses and the more you break them in your own life, the more you will see a difference. Many people do not know how good life can be without the junk because they have always had the junk. They have lived with the junk, put up with the junk, made friends with the junk. They do not know how to get rid of it. To survive, they have made friends with their curses.

All of us have done it. We have assimilated our curses, and we have accommodated them. We have learned to live with them. We say to ourselves, "That's just the way it is. That's how Dad was. That's how Grandpa was. That's how Great-Grandpa was too. That's just the way I am. Everybody in the family as far back as we know has always had this problem with anger, and I have it, too. All the men in the family have always had this lust problem, and I guess I have it, too."

But it is not true that you have to walk in the same footsteps. You have right as a child of God to end the curse in this generation. You can kick the devil in the teeth and get free, in Jesus's name!

Breaking curses is easy. All you have to do is break them. Just say it's so. Declare it done. Break it the way you got it. You have to walk in the Word. You have to walk in the things of the Lord. You have to continue to be faithful and claim His promises and stand by faith. But the actual breaking of the curse is a simple declaration. You just say so. It is really that easy.

When people declare a curse broken, they do not always feel anything immediately. Just as when you got saved, you may not have felt anything immediately after breaking a curse. You need to stand on the Word; confess with your mouth and believe in your heart (see Romans 10:9).

As you read your way through the curse breaking prayers and renunciations at the end of this book, relax and let whatever happens happen. If you feel something start to bubble up on the inside, let it bubble. If you feel something about to be released, let it be released. If you feel something about to react, just let it react, and God will deal with it. You're putting the devil on notice. By reading this book about breaking curses, you have been making him angry and upset. Any demons who have been lurking in your life start to get miserable when they are about to be vanquished by the power of God.

Persist, confident in the power that God supplies. With His help, you can turn your life around. God Himself wants to turn all of your curses into blessings (see Deuteronomy 23:5)—because He loves you!

PRACTICAL
RESOURCES TO
BREAK CURSES

FIVE FACTS ABOUT CURSES

FACT: CURSES ARE TRANSFERABLE

They cannot be "caught" like a virus, but they can be acquired involuntarily through traumas and ill-will directed toward someone. They may be implicit or explicit (unintentional or intentional). Curses are trans-generational. They can be inherited chronologically from one generation to another. This happens even when they are not manifested in a particular generation. They are also intra-generational, meaning that they can be acquired from an individual's present extended family or soul-tie relationships.

FACT: CURSES HAVE CONTINUITY

Continued transference of a curse through inheritance can only be stopped by decisive, Christ-directed action on the part of someone in the current generation. In other words, curses are perpetually invoked—until they are broken. "A curse isn't broken until it is broken." Never fear. Once they are broken, that's the end of the curse, but the negative behavioral patterns caused by the curse must be corrected by modifying one's actions.

FACT: CURSES ARE ADAPTABLE

One of the reasons curses have such longevity is because they are adaptable. Sometimes they leapfrog over an entire generation, most often because it is a godly one. Given an opportunity (by sinful behavior), they can come back to life after lying dormant for a long time. That is why everyone should undergo some degree of curse breaking, no matter how good or godly one's recent ancestors may have lived.

FACT: CURSES ARE SPECIFIC

Curses are attached to very specific conditions, and sometimes they cannot be completely broken without undoing each attachment. To discover the specifics about a curse, ask who, how, what, when, where, and why:

- *Who?* Who created the curse? Was it an ancestor or an unrelated person?

- *How?* How was the curse created? Was it from a ceremonial (ritual) cause or a genetic (ancestral) one? Was it by bloodline or by fiat (a declarative, commanding act of the will)?

- *What?* What is the nature of the curse? (e.g., death, sexual problems, poverty, ill health)

- *When?* When was the curse invoked? Was it invoked recently by a person who is still alive or someone who is now deceased? Is this person known to the victim, or is his or her identity lost in the distant past?

- *Where?* What is the geographical location of the original curse? Knowing the geographical roots of a curse gives clues into its nature.

- *Why?* What harm was intended by this curse? (e.g., to pass on a psychic gift, to victimize sexually, to create a death obsession)

FACT: "THE CAUSELESS CURSE DOES NOT ALIGHT"

The devil can only activate curses based on true causes, and maledictions cannot land on people as curses just because their enemies hate them.

"Like the sparrow in her wandering, like the swallow in her flying, so the causeless curse does not alight" (Prov. 26:2 AMP). "An undeserved curse has no effect" (Prov. 26:2 TLB). After going through the curse breaking procedures of this book, it is important to live a consistent Christian life of worship, study, fellowship, and accountability to keep from providing any "cause" for a curse to be efficacious.

SCRIPTURES ABOUT CURSES

FROM THE OLD TESTAMENT

*So the Lord God said to the serpent: "Because you have done this, you are **cursed** more than all cattle, and more than every beast of the field; on your belly you shall go, and you shall eat dust all the days of your life...." Then to Adam He said, "Because you have heeded the voice of your wife, and have eaten from the tree of which I commanded you, saying, 'You shall not eat of it': **Cursed** is the ground for your sake; in toil you shall eat of it all the days of your life"* (Genesis 3:14, 17).

*Noah awoke from his wine, and knew what his younger son had done to him. Then he said: "**Cursed** be Canaan; a servant of servants he shall be to his brethren"* (Genesis 9:24-25).

*"What if my father touches me? I would appear to be tricking him and would bring down a **curse** on myself rather than a blessing." His mother said to him, "My son, let the **curse** fall on me. Just do what I say; go and get them for me"* (Genesis 27:12-13 NIV).

Isaac said to Jacob, "Please come near, that I may feel you, my son, whether you are really my son Esau or not.... Let peoples serve you, and nations bow down to you. Be master over your brethren, and let your mother's sons bow down to you. **Cursed** *be everyone who* **curses** *you, and blessed be those who bless you"* (Genesis 27:21, 29).

You shall not bow down to them or worship them; for I, the Lord your God, am a jealous God, **punishing** *the children for the sin of the parents to the third and fourth generation of those who hate me* (Exodus 20:5 NIV).

And he passed in front of Moses, proclaiming, "The Lord, the Lord, the compassionate and gracious God, slow to anger, abounding in love and faithfulness, maintaining love to thousands, and forgiving wickedness, rebellion and sin. Yet he does not leave the guilty unpunished; he **punishes** *the children and their children for the sin of the parents to the third and fourth generation"* (Exodus 34:6-7 NIV).

And the priest shall put her under oath, and say to the woman, "If no man has lain with you, and if you have not gone astray to uncleanness while under your husband's authority, be free from this bitter water that brings a **curse.** *But if you have gone astray while under your husband's authority, and if you have defiled yourself and some man other than your husband has lain with you"—then the priest shall put the woman under the oath of the* **curse,** *and he shall say to the woman—"the Lord make you a* **curse** *and an oath among your people, when the Lord makes your thigh rot and your belly swell; and may this water that causes the* **curse** *go into your stomach, and make your belly swell and your thigh rot."*

Then the woman shall say, "Amen, so be it."

Then the priest shall write these **curses** *in a book, and he shall scrape them off into the bitter water. And he shall make the woman drink the bitter water that brings a* **curse,** *and the water that brings the* **curse** *shall enter her to become bitter.... When he has made her drink the water, then it shall be, if* *she has defiled herself and behaved unfaithfully toward her husband, that the water that brings a **curse** will enter her and become bitter, and her belly will swell, her thigh will rot, and the woman will become a **curse** among her people. But if the woman has not defiled herself, and is clean, then she shall be free and may conceive children* (Numbers 5:19-24, 27-28).

*Now Balak the son of Zippor saw all that Israel had done to the Amorites. And Moab was exceedingly afraid of the people because they were many, and Moab was sick with dread because of the children of Israel. So Moab said to the elders of Midian, "Now this company will lick up everything around us, as an ox licks up the grass of the field." And Balak the son of Zippor was king of the Moabites at that time. Then he sent messengers to Balaam the son of Beor at Pethor, which is near the River in the land of the sons of his people, to call him, saying: "Look, a people has come from Egypt. See, they cover the face of the earth, and are settling next to me! Therefore please come at once, **curse** this people for me, for they are too mighty for me. Perhaps I shall be able to defeat them and drive them out of the land, for I know that he whom you bless is blessed, and he whom you **curse** is **cursed**."*

*...And God said to Balaam, "You shall not go with them; you shall not **curse** the people, for they are blessed."*

*...And he took up his oracle and said: "Balak the king of Moab has brought me from Aram, from the mountains of the east. 'Come, **curse** Jacob for me, and come, denounce Israel!' "How shall I **curse** whom God has not **cursed**? And how shall I denounce whom the Lord has not denounced?*

*...Then Balak said to Balaam, "What have you done to me? I took you to **curse** my enemies, and look, you have blessed them bountifully!"*

So he answered and said, "Must I not take heed to speak what the Lord has put in my mouth?"

*...Then Balak's anger was aroused against Balaam, and he struck his hands together; and Balak said to Balaam, "I called you to **curse** my enemies, and look, you have bountifully blessed them these three times* (Numbers 22:2-6, 12; 23:7-8, 11-12; 24:10).

Neither shall you bring an abomination (an idol) *into your house, lest you become an **accursed** thing like it; but you shall utterly detest and abhor it, for it is an **accursed** thing* (Deuteronomy 7:26 AMP).

[Three curses:] No one who has been emasculated by crushing or cutting may enter the assembly of the Lord.

No one born of a forbidden marriage nor any of their descendants may enter the assembly of the Lord, even down to the tenth generation.

*No Ammonite or Moabite or any of their descendants may enter the assembly of the Lord, even down to the tenth generation. For they did not come to meet you with bread and water on your way when you came out of Egypt, and they hired Balaam son of Beor from Pethor in Aram Naharaim to pronounce a **curse** on you* (Deuteronomy 23:1-3 NIV).

*And you, by all means abstain from the **accursed** things, lest you become **accursed** when you take of the **accursed** things, and make the camp of Israel a **curse,** and trouble it* (Joshua 6:18).

*But the children of Israel committed a trespass regarding the **accursed** things, for Achan the son of Carmi, the son of Zabdi, the son of Zerah, of the tribe of Judah, took of the **accursed** things; so the anger of the Lord burned against the children of Israel* (Joshua 7:1).

*Did not Achan the son of Zerah commit a trespass in the **accursed** thing, and wrath fell on all the congregation of Israel? And that man did not perish alone in his iniquity* (Joshua 22:20).

*So the Philistine [Goliath] said to David, "Am I a dog, that you come to me with sticks?" And the Philistine **cursed** David by his gods* (1 Samuel 17:43).

*On that day they read from the Book of Moses in the hearing of the people, and in it was found written that no Ammonite or Moabite should ever come into the assembly of God, because they had not met the children of Israel with bread and water, but hired Balaam against them to **curse** them. However, our God turned the **curse** into a blessing* (Nehemiah 13:1-2).

*You rebuke the proud—the **cursed**, who stray from Your commandments* (Psalm 119:21).

*Do not envy the oppressor, and choose none of his ways; for the perverse person is an abomination to the Lord, but His secret counsel is with the upright. The **curse** of the Lord is on the house of the wicked, but He blesses the home of the just* (Proverbs 3:31-33).

*Like the sparrow in her wandering, like the swallow in her flying, so the causeless **curse** does not alight* (Proverbs 26:2 AMP).

*Are there not still treasures gained by wickedness in the house of the wicked, and a scant measure [a false measure for grain] that is abominable and **accursed**?* (Micah 6:10 AMP).

Then I turned and raised my eyes, and saw there a flying scroll. And he said to me, "What do you see?"

So I answered, "I see a flying scroll. Its length is twenty cubits and its width ten cubits."

*Then he said to me, "This is the **curse** that goes out over the face of the whole earth: 'Every thief shall be expelled,' according to this side of the scroll; and, 'Every perjurer shall be expelled,' according to that side of it."*

*"I will send out the **curse**," says the Lord of hosts;*

"It shall enter the house of the thief and the house of the one who swears falsely by My name. It shall remain in the midst of his house and consume it, with its timber and stones."

Then the angel who talked with me came out and said to me, "Lift your eyes now, and see what this is that goes forth" (Zechariah 5:1-5).

If you do not listen, and if you do not resolve to honor my name," says the Lord Almighty, *"I will send a **curse** on you, and I will **curse** your blessings. Yes, I have already **cursed** them, because you have not set your heart to honor me"* (Malachi 2:2 NIV).

*Will a man rob God? Yet you have robbed Me! But you say, "In what way have we robbed You?" In tithes and offerings. You are **cursed** with a **curse**, for you have robbed Me, even this whole nation* (Malachi 3:8-9).

FROM THE NEW TESTAMENT

A good man brings good things out of the good stored up in him, and an evil man brings evil things out of the evil stored up in him (Matthew 12:35 NIV).

Now the next day, when they had come out from Bethany, He was hungry. And seeing from afar a fig tree having leaves, He went to see if perhaps He would find something on it. When He came to it, He found nothing but leaves, for it was not the season for figs. In response Jesus said to it, "Let no one eat fruit from you ever again."

And His disciples heard it....

*Now in the morning, as they passed by, they saw the fig tree dried up from the roots. And Peter, remembering, said to Him, "Rabbi, look! The fig tree which You **cursed** has withered away"* (Mark 11:12-14, 20).

When the Son of Man comes in His glory, and all the holy angels with Him, then He will sit on the throne of His glory. All the nations will be gathered before Him, and He will separate them one from another, as a shepherd divides his sheep from the goats. And He will set the sheep on His right hand, but the goats on the left. Then the King will say to those on His right hand, "Come, you blessed of My Father, inherit the kingdom prepared for you from the foundation of the world...."

Then He will also say to those on the left hand, "Depart from Me, you **cursed***, into the everlasting fire prepared for the devil and his angels: for I was hungry and you gave Me no food; I was thirsty and you gave Me no drink; I was a stranger and you did not take Me in, naked and you did not clothe Me, sick and in prison and you did not visit Me"* (Matthew 25:31-34, 41-43).

Then Peter began to invoke a **curse** *on himself and to swear, I do not even know the Man! And at that moment a rooster crowed* (Matt. 26:74 AMP, see also Mark 14:71).

For Moses said, "Honor your father and your mother"; and, "He who **curses** *father or mother, let him be put to death"* (Mark 7:10).

But I say to you who hear: Love your enemies, do good to those who hate you, bless those who **curse** *you, and pray for those who spitefully use you* (Luke 6:27-28).

Finally the temple guards went back to the chief priests and the Pharisees, who asked them, "Why didn't you bring him in?"

"No one ever spoke the way this man does," the guards declared.

"You mean he has deceived you also?" the Pharisees retorted. "Have any of the rulers or of the Pharisees believed in him? No! But this mob that knows nothing of the law—there is a curse on them" (John 7:45-49 NIV).

And [that same] following night the Lord stood beside Paul and said, Take courage, Paul, for as you have borne faithful witness concerning Me at Jerusalem, so you must also bear witness at Rome.

*Now when daylight came, the Jews formed a plot and bound themselves by an oath and under a **curse** neither to eat nor drink till they had done away with Paul. There were more than forty [men of them], who formed this conspiracy [swearing together this oath and **curse**]* (Acts 23:11-13 AMP).

*I have great sorrow and continual grief in my heart. For I could wish that I myself were **accursed** from Christ for my brethren, my countrymen according to the flesh, who are Israelites...* (Romans 9:2-4).

*To this very hour we go hungry and thirsty, we are in rags, we are brutally treated, we are homeless. We work hard with our own hands. When we are **cursed**, we bless; when we are persecuted, we endure it; when we are slandered, we answer kindly* (1 Corinthians 4:11-13 NIV).

*If anyone does not love the Lord Jesus Christ, let him be **accursed**. O Lord, come* (1 Corinthians 16:22).

*But even if we or an angel from heaven should preach a gospel other than the one we preached to you, let them be under God's **curse**. As we have already said, so now I say again: If anybody is preaching to you a gospel other than what you accepted, let them be under God's **curse*** (Galatians 1:8-9 NIV).

*For as many as are of the works of the law are under the **curse**; for it is written, "**Cursed** is everyone who does not continue in all things which are written in the book of the law, to do them." But that no one is justified by the law in the sight of God is evident, for "the just shall live by faith." Yet the law is not of faith, but "the man who does them shall live by them."*

*Christ has redeemed us from the **curse** of the law, having become a **curse** for us (for it is written, "**Cursed** is everyone who hangs on a tree"), that the blessing of Abraham might come upon the Gentiles in Christ Jesus, that we might receive the promise of the Spirit through faith* (Galatians 3:10-14).

*They are spots and blemishes, carousing in their own deceptions while they feast with you, having eyes full of adultery and that cannot cease from sin, enticing unstable souls. They have a heart trained in covetous practices, and are **accursed** children* (2 Peter 2:13-14).

*And there shall be no more **curse**, but the throne of God and of the Lamb shall be in it, and His servants shall serve Him* (Revelation 22:3).

Basic Curse-Breaking Prayers and Renunciations

Our DWJD (Do What Jesus Did) healing and deliverance teams have found that having a person read the following curse breaking document out loud to break this long list of curses off their lives is a very useful first step in the process of freedom from spiritual oppression. Getting some initial relief by means of this curse breaking process can accelerate the overall results of deliverance. As curse breaking is done, the following are important factors to consider:

1. The person should have a Christian confession, because curses are broken in Jesus's name.

2. People must believe what they are saying as they confess it with their mouths. (See Romans 10:9-10.)

3. Certain racial, ethnic, and geographical backgrounds may require more specific curse breaking.

Introductory Prayer

Heavenly Father, I come before you now to ask forgiveness for the curses of my ancestors and those curses that I have brought on my own life. I beseech you Lord, on behalf of the ancestors in my father and mother's lineage going all the way back to Adam and Eve. As I speak and declare each confession, I pray that you would forgive me and my ancestors and put these sins under the blood of my Lord and Savior, Jesus Christ of Nazareth. I pray that you would break these curses on both sides of my family, including any ancestors of my spouse or ex-spouse(s). Inasmuch as some of my descendants are not yet of legal age, I break all these curses on their behalf. Whoever of my descendants is already of legal age must break these curses by their own renunciation.

BREAKING THE CURSE OF FALSE RELIGION

In the name of Jesus, I renounce and break all curses of false religion that are on me and future generations. This renunciation includes, but is not limited to, the following curses:

1. False religion, doctrinal error, dogma, legalism, unbelief, doubt, rejection of God, anger at God, unbelief in God's Word as Holy-Spirit-inspired truth, unbelief in God's power, unbelief that Jesus Christ is God, unbelief in Christ's death and resurrection, unbelief in the finished work of Jesus at Calvary, rejection of grace, striving to win God's love, striving to reach holiness and perfection in one's own efforts, striving to reach Heaven based on merit and good works.

2. Hypocrisy, religious bondage, religious slavery, religious murder, lust and ambition for recognition, lust and ambition for position, lust and ambition for power and control in religious matters, Jezebel and Ahab, false love, false gifts, false tongues, false discernment, false words of wisdom, false prophecy, religious dominance, false laying on of hands, selfishness, greed, religious apathy, lack of compassion, pretense, false oaths, rigid theology, hatred of truth, anti-Semitism, anti-Catholicism, anti-Protestantism, judgmental attitudes, lying, gossip, slander, division, criticism, stealing, schisms, and backbiting.

3. Aetherius Society, Native American religions, Ascended Masters, Assembly of Yahweh, Edgar Cayce, Baha'i Faith, black magic, Buddhism, Christian Science, Church Universal and Triumphant, *A Course in Miracles*, Eckankar, est (Erhard Seminars Training), Esalen, Hinduism, Mormonism, New Age, Rastafarianism, Rosicrucianism, Kabbalah, Self-Realization Fellowship, Swedenborgianism, TM (Transcendental Meditation), obsession with UFOs, Unification Church, Unitarian Universalist Association, macumba, voodoo, Santeria, Islam, Krishna Consciousness, Theosophy, Religious Science (Science of Mind), Scientology, Jehovah's Witnesses, mind control, yoga, and all false Christian sects.

4. I cut all soul ties with the founders, teachers, and proponents of these religions and renounce all demons attached to these religions and their leaders. I cancel every ritual, ceremony, and blood covenant associated with these false belief systems.

BREAKING THE CURSE OF WITCHCRAFT

In the name of Jesus, I renounce and break all curses of witchcraft on me and future generations. This renunciation includes, but is not limited to, the following curses:

1. All evil curses, fetishes, charms, vexes, hexes, spells, jinxes; all psychic powers, sorcery, enchantments, witchcraft, and love spells.

2. Any spirits connected with any person or persons from any occult practice or psychic source.

3. All psychic heredity gifts, demonic strongholds, psychic powers, bondage of physical and mental illness, family and marital rebellion and strife, sins, transgressions, iniquities, or occult and psychic involvement.

4. All forms of divination and seeking guidance through witchcraft and occult practices, including: Ouija Board, charming, séances, scrying, necromancy, crystal balls, phrenology, palm-reading, astrology and influence of personal birth sign, horoscopes, fortune-telling, false dreams, runes; reading coffee grounds and tea leaves, dripped wax, or bones.

5. All involvement in table-tipping, "light as a feather, stiff as a board" (party levitation), Bloody Mary summons, crystals, automatic writing or painting, channeling, pagan festivals, sorcery, spells, incantations, curses, magic (black and white), water-witching, dowsing, witchcraft, Wicca, spell books, or love potions.

6. Worship of mother earth or earth goddess, spiritism, spiritualism, secret oaths, superstitions, demonic role-playing games, vows; belief in fairies, native spirits, or spirit guides.

7. Participation of my ancestors in occult or satanic rituals including orgies, temple prostitution, annual sacrifices, animal or human sacrifices, worship of idols, ceremonies honoring false gods and goddesses, covenants to false gods, self-mutilation, or bacchanalian parties.

8. Luciferian, satanic, and Freemasonry curses, and all secret society bondage.

9. I cut all soul ties with those living and dead who have enticed me or my ancestors into these witchcraft indulgences. I cut off their future access to me through the psychic third eye, the opening of any chakras, communication by channeling, books, seminars, objects such as crystals or amulets, dissociated soul transference, astral projection, mind control, manipulation of alters through triggers, or any other open door. Every open door via

my mind and soul is hereby closed through the blood of Christ and all access denied from this point forward.

BREAKING THE CURSE OF DESTRUCTIVE EMOTIONS #1

In the name of Jesus, I renounce and break all curses of destructive emotions on me and future generations. This renunciation includes, but is not limited to, the following curses:

Pride

1. All forms of pride, including a "stiff neck," pride of life, physical pride, intellectual pride, spiritual pride, disdainful haughtiness, pretense of inferiority, arrogance, smugness, cunning, trickery, deceit, and all lies.

2. I specifically renounce the spirit of Leviathan, the King of Pride, and remove any crown of pride he has placed on me.

3. I break any inordinate opinion of myself related to a false sense of dignity or merit. I ask the Holy Spirit to show me the difference between appropriate self-esteem and the error of false superiority. I ask that all I do be for the glory of Christ alone.

So whether you eat or drink or whatever you do, do it all for the glory of God (1 Corinthians 10:31 NIV).

Rejection

1. I renounce and break all curses of rejection, perceived rejection, rejection from word curses, rejection in the womb, all inner vows I have spoken, and bitter-root judgments I have uttered over myself.

2. I renounce and break all curses of verbal and relational rejection of my parents and their ancestors.

3. I renounce and break all curses of falsely perceived rejection by God; rejection resulting from mental, physical, verbal, and sexual abuse.

4. I renounce and break all curses of resentment, bitterness, anger, jealousy, envy, unforgiveness, grief, shame, and false guilt resulting from rejection.

5. I also renounce all abandonment that resulted in the spirit of rejection.

BREAKING THE CURSE OF DESTRUCTIVE EMOTIONS #2

In the name of Jesus, I renounce and break all curses of destructive emotions that are on me and future generations. This renunciation includes, but is not limited to, the following curses:

Anger and Hate

1. Unforgiveness, rage, seething anger, fury, revengeful hate.

2. Hatred of father, mother, spouse, ex-spouse, all prior sexual and emotional and soul-tie relationships. Hatred of men, of women, of spiritual leaders, of those in authority in the Church and in civil government.

3. I renounce all connected emotions of self-hate, impulsiveness, irritation, wrath, temper tantrums, contention, strife, conflict, immature self-will, violence, fighting, or war.

4. I renounce and break all curses of racial hatred; hatred of countries, of political parties, of ethnic identities.

5. I renounce all hatred toward those who have tormented me, abused me, or treated me harshly.

And when you stand praying, if you hold anything against anyone, forgive him, so that your Father in heaven may forgive you your sins (Mark 11:25 NIV).

Fear

1. I renounce and break all curses related to the fear of giving and receiving love freely.

2. I renounce and break all curses of the fear of death, of darkness, of animals, and of all living creatures; fear of crowds, of water, of choking, of drowning, of sexual assault, of close places, of storms, and fear of the future.

3. I renounce and break all curses related to the fear of demons, of Satan, of the loss of salvation, and of judgment. This includes the false fear of hell, as well as false fear of the Holy Spirit, Jesus, and God.

4. I renounce and break all curses related to the fear of other people: fear of men or of women, fear of childbearing, fear of relationships, fear of marriage, and fear of spiritual leadership.

5. I renounce and break all curses related to nightmares, insomnia or night terrors; to fear of torment, torture, trauma, terror, dreams, or accidents; to superstitions, agoraphobia, and all irrational phobias.

For God has not given us a spirit of fear, but of power and of love and of a sound mind (2 Timothy 1:7).

BREAKING THE CURSE OF DESTRUCTIVE EMOTIONS #3

In the name of Jesus, I renounce and break all curses of destructive emotions that are on me and future generations. This renunciation includes, but is not limited to, the following curses:

Depression

1. Depression, hopelessness, despair, despondency, worthlessness, a broken heart, a wounded spirit, and all accompanying thoughts of death, suicide, self-harm, and self-destruction.

2. All forms of mental illness and emotional incapacitation associated with depression, including schizophrenia, paranoia, bipolar disorder (manic depression), borderline personality disorder, lunacy, insanity, and similar emotional disturbances.

3. I renounce and break all curses related to negative responses to depression and trauma such as addictions to alcohol, drugs, gambling and pornography; obsessive compulsive disorder, anxiety disorders, and post-traumatic stress disorder.

4. I renounce and break all curses related to physical responses to depression and trauma, which may include dementia, senility, neurological damage, epilepsy, seizures, convulsions, all hormonal and chemical imbalances, and self-abuse.

Hope deferred makes the heart sick, but a longing fulfilled is a tree of life (Proverbs 13:12 NIV).

Isolation

1. I renounce and break all curses related to isolation, loneliness, unnatural grief, agoraphobia, and all unwarranted religious justifications for emotional separation.

2. I renounce and break all curses related to a wandering spirit, a relationally dysfunctional lifestyle, idleness and sloth leading to inactivity.

3. I renounce every false rationalization to justify friendlessness, lack of Christian community, of fellowship, of mentors, and of accountability.

4. I renounce every demonic force with an assignment from Satan to "keep me to himself" and away from the Lord, family, and caring spiritual leaders.

5. I renounce each plan of Satan to keep me divorced, unmarried, single, without even platonic connections, and fearful of trusting and being emotionally vulnerable.

BREAKING THE CURSE OF DESTRUCTIVE EMOTIONS #4

In the name of Jesus, I renounce and break all curses of destructive emotions that are on me and future generations. This renunciation includes, but is not limited to, the following curses:

Self-Hatred

1. Self-hate, self-abuse, self-condemnation (as evidenced by being guilt-ridden, feeling like a failure, filled with thoughts of insufficiency and self-loathing).

2. I renounce negative voices from my past (such as verbal and emotional abuse from parents, pastors, teachers, Christian leaders, and friends).

3. I renounce the voice inside telling me I am no good, I'll never amount to anything, I'd be better off dead, I should do the world a favor and kill myself, no one will ever love and accept me, I'll always be a failure, and that even God doesn't want me.

4. I renounce condemning thoughts that attack my physical appearance, my intellectual skills, my emotional capacities, and my relationship with God (questioning my worthiness to be saved by God's grace).

5. I renounce and break all curses related to every destructive impulse to self-harm through cutting or other forms of self-injurious abuse. I reject every suggestion

of sudden death, suicide, running away, hiding, or allowing my thoughts to entertain unhealthy fantasies or delusions.

Addiction

1. I renounce and break all curses related to every form of narcissism and self-absorption leading to addictions to drugs, alcohol, gambling, lust, gluttony, bulimia, anorexia, bingeing and purging.

2. I renounce and reject all spirits of Deception, Stupor, Cravings, Compulsions, Hangover, Hallucinations, Slow Death, and Dishonoring the Body (which is the temple of the Holy Spirit).

3. I renounce and reject all cravings and unnatural desires for damaging indulgences including psychoactive and psychotropic drugs (both prescription and recreational, legal and illegal), which are unnecessary to life, health, and pain management.

4. I renounce and break all curses related to marijuana, speed, LSD, hallucinogens, heroin, crack, designer drugs, barbiturates, crank, PCP, all non-medical opiates, cocaine, methadone, sniffing solvents, unnecessary sleep aids; along with all illegal peddling, trafficking, or the formulating of such addictive, unlicensed drugs.

BREAKING THE CURSE OF DESTRUCTIVE EMOTIONS #5

In the name of Jesus, I renounce and break all curses of destructive emotions that are on me and future generations. This renunciation includes, but is not limited to, the following curses:

Lust

1. I renounce and reject all lust, lust of the flesh, pornography, unclean conversations and fantasies, tormenting dreams, sinful imaginations and flashbacks, sexualized memories, unwholesome fantasies, a wandering eye, ungodly flirtation.

2. I renounce and break all curses related to illicit sexually-related activities including adultery, infidelity, immorality, fornication, promiscuity, molestation, rape, incest, prostitution, procuring prostitutes, stripping, going to strip clubs, compulsive masturbation; as well as viewing pornographic movies, television, magazines, videos, and Internet.

3. I renounce and break all curses related to perversion, bestiality, pedophilia, sexual violence and cruelty, masochism, sadomasochism, tantric sex, or occult sex. I renounce all spirits of Harlotry and Whoredom, Uncleanness, Defilement, Lewdness, Lasciviousness, Nudity, Voyeurism, Incubus, or Succubus.

4. I renounce and break all curses related to activity affecting sexual relationships, including frigidity, impotence, sterility, infertility, unfulfilled relationships, multiple divorces, and failed marriages.

5. I renounce and reject all entrance of sexual demons through any bodily orifices, including ears, eyes, nose (smell), touch; as well as through dreams, visualizations, nocturnal arousal, daydreaming, or any demonic sexual stimulation.

6. I renounce and break all curses related to illicit relationships before or after marriage and all soul ties associated with such relationships.

7. I renounce and break all curses related to attempts to use sex to obtain power, wealth, control, domination, and manipulation of relationships.

8. I renounce and reject all attempts of Satan to instill false shame, false guilt, self-condemnation, self-hatred, shame or hatred of my body. I renounce and break all curses related to false attempts at purity and self-isolation through weight gain, unkept appearance, anorexia/bulimia, or offensive behavior.

BREAKING THE CURSE OF DESTRUCTIVE EMOTIONS #6

In the name of Jesus, I renounce and break all curses of destructive emotions that are on me and future generations. This renunciation includes, but is not limited to, the following curses:

Rebellion

1. Rebellion against God, disobedience, a lukewarm attitude; spiritual disregard, apathy and lethargy; any form of idolatry (including worshipping false gods or idolatrous behavior), self-righteousness, feigned spirituality, and the spirit of Jezebel.

2. I repent and renounce rebellious behavior and break all curses that may have come with my rebellion, specifically: refusal to submit to authority (to my parents before my legal emancipation), to my husband (if I am a wife), or to the pastor or spiritual elders of my church. I renounce and break all curses associated with rebellion regarding civil affairs and established governmental authority, including law-breaking and failure to pay taxes, rioting, theft, anarchism, nihilism, violent civil disobedience.

3. I renounce and break all curses associated with rebellion-related emotions and attitudes, including being unteachable, defensive, argumentative, subversive, manipulative, controlling, or demanding; also making a pretense of submission, coercion, and setting my own agenda in conflict with the common good.

BREAKING THE CURSE OF DEMONIC BEHAVIOR #1

In the name of Jesus, I renounce and break all curses of demonic behavior that are on me and future generations. This renunciation includes, but is not limited to, the following curses:

Curses of National, Ethnic, and Racial Origin

1. I revoke all generational curses, demonic genealogies, racial depravity, and corrupted nationalities that came through my bloodline. This renunciation applies to me and all future generations. I repent on behalf of the sins and iniquities of all my ancestors going back to Adam and Eve, including all of their ungodly oaths, vows, and ceremonial acts and rituals involving the worship of false gods, goddesses, and idols. I ask forgiveness for all bloodshed and every blood covenant with sacrifices of animals or human beings.

2. I renounce and break all curses of prejudice (both racial or ethnic superiority and racial or ethnic inferiority). I rebuke and renounce all spirits associated with conquest, rape, pillage, domination, genocide, theft of land or property, murder, attack, the taking of territories by violence; the killing of families, households, villages and nations.

3. I renounce and break all curses of slavery, oppression, injustice; and any nationalistic desire to conquer for wealth, power, prestige, and subjugation.

4. I rebuke the demons of War, Violence, Antichrist, Abaddon, Apollyon, Molech, and Nike.

Murder

1. I renounce and break all curses of murder, revenge, retaliation, jealousy, abortion, self-harm, self-cutting, suicide, suicide attempts, suicidal thoughts, infanticide, worship of Molech, child sacrifice, fratricide, birth control destroying fertilized eggs, and ritual murder or gang murder.

2. I repent of all destructive thoughts or actions toward properties, people, institutions, civil and religious leaders, and those who have wronged me or treated me unjustly; all plans, speculations, or musings about vengeance by causing physical or emotional hurt. I break all curses related to such thoughts or actions.

3. I break all curses incurred by any ancestor who committed acts of murder or attempted murder, and all past instances within my family line of violence or instigation of violence leading to harm of any kind.

BREAKING THE CURSE OF DEMONIC BEHAVIOR #2

In the name of Jesus, I renounce and break all curses of demonic behavior that are on me and future generations. This renunciation includes, but is not limited to, the following curses:

Death and Destruction

1. Each and every death wish for myself or others; any blood oaths, vows, or blood covenants, including sexual rituals of vampirism or blood-sharing.

2. I renounce and break all curses stemming from involvement in the occult, witchcraft, voodoo, revenge magic,

and divination, where such involvement led to scheming or plotting to murder any child (infanticide) or the killing of family members (brothers, sisters, parents and all other relatives).

3.   I renounce and break all curses that have resulted from desiring the death of any person; or from wishing injury to someone's career, future, destiny, relationships, blessings, happiness, spiritual life, joy, freedom, honor, marriage, spiritual riches, prosperity, purpose, creativity, design, or goals.

4.   I renounce and break all curses that have resulted from participation in any crime, including stealing, vandalism, graffiti, looting, arson, anarchy, malice with evil intent, destruction of goods or property, harming or showing disrespect for the property or possessions of others.

Amusements

1.   I renounce and break all curses that have come from ungodly pastimes of gambling, alcoholism, or demonic entertainment; hedonistic lifestyles, lascivious amusements, and profane music; tattoos, body piercing, orgies, drunkenness, vice, revelry, and all unwholesome activities.

2.   I repent for attending or visiting any demonic ceremonies, pagan rituals, vulgar concerts, gambling casinos, irreverent movies and theatrical productions, and any blasphemous or sacrilegious indulgence, and I break any curses that have resulted from these activities.

Finances

1.   I repent for the love of money, greed, covetousness, theft, stealing, and using unjust scales or balances, and I break all curses associated with this sinful behavior. I renounce

a spirit of Poverty, Lack, not enjoying the fruits of one's labor, failure to pay tithes, failure to pay taxes, and I break all curses associated with this mindset. I also break the curse from Malachi for robbing God (see Malachi 3:8-9) and the curse of pests devouring "crops" and the "fruit" of my "fields," having renounced the unvirtuous behavior that led to these curses.

2.   I agree to pay all my back taxes and tithes as I am able, to make restitution of anything I have stolen, and to conduct my financial affairs in an honest and just way.

3.   I resist every spirit of Poverty and Lack and demonic withholding of my finances and demand a sevenfold return, according to the law of restitution. (See Proverbs 6:31.)

BREAKING THE CURSE OF DEMONIC BEHAVIOR #3

In the name of Jesus, I renounce and break all curses of demonic behavior that are on me and future generations. This renunciation includes, but is not limited to, the following curses:

The Spirit of Jezebel/Ahab

1.   The spirit of Jezebel and/or Ahab represented by murder, control, false submission, manipulation, arrogance, false spirituality, unaccountability; and all the forms in which Jezebel operates, such as Queen of Heaven, Queen of Babylon, wife, mother, mentor, lover, sexual partner, teacher, pastor, leader.

2.   I renounce all Jezebel/Ahab involvement in every relationship, such as husband-wife, mother-child, father-child, pastor-lay person, employer-employee, friend-friend, mentor-student, lover-lover (including the use of sex to

manipulate); and I repent of using power, money, or position to corrupt such relationships.

3. I renounce and repent of all hatred and rebellion toward men, authority, Christian leadership; and all forms of expression of this hatred and rebellion, including a sharp tongue, sexual seduction, anger, and pretended cooperation.

4. I renounce every way that the spirit of Jezebel and/or Ahab operates, including, but not limited to, barrenness, infertility, despising of children, irreverence toward holy things, gossip, backbiting, undermining leadership, destroying marriages, deviously attacking spiritual leaders, inciting spiritual failure or church schisms, questioning biblical authority, misogyny, perpetrating emotional castration, and fostering witchcraft and rebellion.

5. I renounce every form of Jezebel's expression through spirits of Lilith, Ashtoreth, Aphrodite, Astarte, Diana, Venus, Ishtar, Isis, Kali, Anat, and other goddess forms throughout history. I renounce all Jezebel's partners and cohorts, including the spirits of Ahab, Molech, Baal, Murder, Witchcraft, and Lucifer. I sever every soul tie with these false gods and false goddesses and every sexual, emotional, or spiritual bond I have forged with any person controlled by Jezebel. In judgment, I release the dogs of Jezreel (see 2 Kings 9:34-37) to spiritually eat the flesh and drink the blood of Jezebel to drive her influence completely from my life.

BREAKING THE CURSE OF PHYSICAL AND MENTAL INFIRMITIES #1

In the name of Jesus, I renounce and break all curses of physical and mental infirmities that are on me and future generations. This renunciation includes, but is not limited to, the following curses:

Infirmities

1. Every genetic and congenital disease passed on by hereditary transference. This includes, but is not limited to, arthritis, cancer, epilepsy, fibromyalgia, gastrointestinal diseases, eyes/ears/nose/throat diseases, heart disease, high blood pressure, pulmonary problems, all diseases of the joints and extremities, skeletal and musculoskeletal diseases, diseases of the lymphatic and endocrine systems, neurological conditions, vascular abnormalities, genital diseases, brain malfunctions, and all disorders of every internal organ.

2. I renounce each and every disease, infirmity, disability, illness, sickness, ailment, abnormal condition, disordered bodily function, infection, nutritional deficiency, and internal toxicity.

3. I renounce every factor influencing my health, including those factors that are pathogenic, parasitic, poisonous, environmental, or caused by microorganisms, viruses, and genetic mutations.

4. I break every curse intended to affect my overall health, bring about death or premature death, result in suffering, increase pain, heighten vulnerability to disease, or cause bodily malfunctions; to bring about wasting, loss of will to live, or fear of dying.

5. I declare the healing of Christ to every physical abnormality or dysfunction and the restoration of my body to health and wholeness.

Mental Health Issues

1. I break every curse associated with all forms of mental illness and emotional incapacitation including schizophrenia, paranoia, depression, bi-polar disorder (manic

depression), borderline personality disorder, lunacy, insanity, and similar mental/emotional disturbances.

2. I renounce all age-related attacks on my mind, including dementia, senility, loss of memory, Alzheimer's, confusion, mental distraction, and forgetfulness.

3. Obsessive-compulsive disorder, panic attacks, post-traumatic stress disorder, agoraphobia, panophobia, narcissism, all anxiety disorders, autism, attention deficit disorder, and hyperactivity disorders.

4. I declare the healing of Christ to every mental health issue and restoration to health and wholeness.

BREAKING THE CURSE OF PHYSICAL AND MENTAL INFIRMITIES #2

In the name of Jesus, I renounce and break all curses of physical and mental infirmities that are on me and future generations. This renunciation includes, but is not limited to, the following curses:

Attacks Upon the Organs

1. All cancer, including cancer of the breast, cancer of the stomach, leukemia and other cancers of the blood, cancer of the prostate, skin cancer, lung cancer, lymphatic cancer, brain cancer, cancer of the reproductive organs, and cancer of the colon and intestines.

2. I rebuke every demonic attack causing tumors, uncontrolled cell growth, strokes, or paralysis; and all diseases including sickle cell anemia, Lou Gehrig's Disease (ALS) and other motor neuron diseases, muscular dystrophy, diabetes, eczema and all other skin diseases, Parkinson's disease, Crohn's disease, multiple sclerosis, AIDS, and all chronic diseases.

3. I renounce and break all curses that have affected the eyes and that have resulted in poor eyesight, including astigmatism, glaucoma, cataracts, detached retina, and any degree of blindness.

4. I renounce and break all curses that have resulted in weight control and eating disorders, including both overeating and undereating.

5. I renounce and break all curses concerning heart issues, including high cholesterol, congestive heart failure, heart murmurs, false cardiac arrests, arrhythmias, heart valve problems, blood clots, phlebitis, hardening and thinning and blocking of the arteries, and all fear of these conditions.

6. I renounce and break all curses concerning pulmonary conditions, including bronchial and lung infections, asthma, emphysema, allergic rhinitis (hay fever), sinusitis, bronchitis, and any other causes of poor lung capacity.

7. I renounce and break all curses concerning skeletal abnormalities, including curvature of the spine, scoliosis, and other bone or joint abnormalities or infirmities.

8. I renounce and break all curses that have resulted in malfunctioning of the liver, skin, pancreas, appendix, reproductive organs, thyroid, gall bladder, kidneys, and any organ that affects the body systemically (affecting the entire body).

9. I renounce and break all curses that cause or intensify chronic pain, including pain of the back and spinal column; pain that results from sprains, muscle tears, and diseased tissue and joints—all pain that inhibits normal activity.

10. I renounce and break all curses concerning cirrhosis, hearing problems, hypoglycemia, ulcers, hepatitis, and

any ailments resulting in swelling, edema, itching, burning, vertigo, paralysis, impotency, sterility, miscarriage, fainting, convulsions, or any other symptom of ill health.

11. By the stripes of Christ (see 1 Peter 2:24) I am healed. All of my cells, all of my DNA, all of my chromosomes, all of my organs, and all of my senses must comply with God's divine order for my being. Every evil spirit assigned to destroy any aspect of my physical body is henceforth bound from causing further torment or harassment.

BREAKING THE CURSE OF FALSE SPIRITUALITY

In the name of Jesus, I renounce and break all curses of false spirituality that are on me and future generations. This renunciation includes, but is not limited to, the following curses:

1. All false religions and religious practices, especially those rooted in the ancient worship of the Sumerians, Babylonians, Egyptians, Assyrians, and Druids.

2. Every false god and false goddess, every deity and demigod, every spirit, demon, idol, icon, object, and amulet.

3. All false religions, including all their rituals, ceremonies, creeds, so-called sacred texts and scrolls, offerings, sacrifices, and covenants, especially blood covenants involving the sacrifice of animals and humans.

4. Further, I renounce and break all curses of false spirituality coming from organizations that promote intellectual and ethical behavior devoid of Judeo-Christianity principles and seek to better humankind by deliberately negating Christ's blood atonement.

5. I renounce every affiliation, commendation, degree, vow, oath, contract, agreement, and ungodly utterance that

stands in competition with or opposed to my commitment to the Father, Son, and Holy Spirit.

6. I renounce every attempt to supplant the wisdom of Christ with demonically influenced philosophies, theories, rationalizations, exalted or false wisdom, or reliance on ascended masters, resulting in the exaltation of the intellect or doctrines of demons.

7. I renounce every false religious leader, guru, teacher, avatar, founder, spokesperson, and representative to whom I have pledged devotion, given gifts and offerings, or with whom I have had sexual or emotional bonding. I break all soul ties associated with these individuals, expel any soul transferences from them, and repudiate all mind control.

8. I repent of and renounce every spoken word on behalf of all false spirituality, including blasphemies, profanities, sacrilege, cursing, death oaths, self-injury vows, secret pacts, and all mockery of Christianity.

9. I renounce and break all curses associated with occult practices including, but not limited to, yoga, TM, tantric practices, guided imagery, visualizations, godless holism, demonic meditation, mind control hypnosis, mantras, chants, reliance on psychic powers, past life therapy, spirit guides and channeling, reincarnation, Qiqong, kundalini, prana, chakras, auras, clairvoyance, ESP, all psychic powers, psychic healing, Reiki, I Ching, and all divination. I also renounce all teachers, facilitators, gurus, and leaders who induced me to indulge these practices and break every soul tie with them. I also break every agreement, seal, covenant, and submission associated with these practices and the individuals who transmitted them to me.

BREAKING THE CURSES OF
ALL SOUL-TIE ISSUES

In the name of Jesus, I renounce and break all curses of all soul-tie issues that are on me and future generations. This renunciation includes, but is not limited to, the following curses:

1. Every unhealthy and ungodly emotional, physical, sexual, mental, psychic, spiritual, professional, relational bond that I have entered into by which I have become tied to another individual, including any friend, family member, lover, ex-lover, spouse, ex-spouse, prostitute, employer, mentor, pastor, or anyone else I have allowed myself to become attached to in a way that has resulted in my detriment.

2. I renounce all emotions, vows, promises, pledges, formal or informal binding agreements that I uttered or entered into with the person to whom I was soul tied or with whom I was in a one-flesh relationship, and I break all curses associated with those relationships.

3. I ask forgiveness for any deception or seduction that led to this bondage. I ask for healing of the memories of all circumstances that led to the soul tie. I forgive the other individual for what he or she may have done to seduce, deceive, or hurt me in any way.

4. If any soul-part of the person to whom I was bonded has been embedded in any part of my mind or emotions, I ask the Holy Spirit to remove it. If any demons are attached to any transferred soul-part, I resist these evil spirits by the blood of Christ. I send those parts back to the person from which they came. I will return or destroy, whichever is appropriate, any objects which connect me to that individual, objects that may remind me of that person or were a gift from that person. By removing these physical

reminders, I am cutting off all ways in which Satan may keep that person in my life.

5. In the name of Jesus, I renounce, resist, and break all curses of shame, guilt, self-condemnation, harassment, stalking, or emotional torment related to this person. As the soul tie is broken, this person no longer has any spiritually legal right to influence my life.

6. Every door in every part of my being that was affected by this soul tie is now closed and sealed by the blood of Christ.

BREAKING THE CURSE OF EVERY FRAGMENTED SOUL

In the name of Jesus, I renounce and break all curses of every fragmented soul that are on me and future generations. This renunciation includes, but is not limited to, the following curses:

1. Every attempt of Satan through witchcraft, satanism, or any occult power to fragment my mind and emotions. I repent of my involvement in practices that may have facilitated this evil intention, such as practicing eastern mysticism, meditation, hypnotherapy, trancing, channeling, or various forms of mind control; taking drugs, or listening to demonic music.

2. I ask the angels of the Lord and the Holy Spirit to capture all the broken parts of my mind and bring them back to me in restoration and wholeness according to Psalm 23:3 ("He restores my soul").

3. I renounce every attempt by any person to control my mind and life and thereby cause my emotions to fragment through their domination. This renunciation includes any unintentional mind control indulged in by

my ancestors, passing on to me the propensity to disassociate negatively.

4.   I ask healing for every psychologically dissociated or emotionally disconnected part of my mind and emotions. While I recognize that temporarily such a condition may facilitate survival after trauma, I know that it is God's will for me not to be "double-minded" but stable in all my thoughts and actions (see James 1:2-7). I want this healing to penetrate every aspect of my soul, even the deepest parts that are subject to amnesia, so that no demonic force can manipulate my condition consciously or unconsciously.

BREAKING THE CURSE OF BIBLICAL ABOMINATIONS

In the name of Jesus, I renounce and break all curses of biblical abominations that are on me and future generations. This renunciation includes, but is not limited to, the following curses:

1.   Every biblical curse pronounced on immoral, disobedient, and ungodly behavior. This includes the curse of illegitimacy (in Deuteronomy 23:2), the curse of anti-Semitism (in Genesis 12:3), and all the curses of which God warns His people in Deuteronomy 28.

2.   All curses of death, isolation, alienation from God, poverty, and every physical and mental consequence of spiritual rebellion.

3.   Every curse of fornication, adultery, incest, sexual perversion, all moral impurities, keeping cursed objects, ignoring the poor, taking advantage of the innocent and vulnerable, witchcraft, thievery, swearing falsely, idolatry, cursing (especially taking the Lord's name in vain), coveting, cheating, dishonesty, failure to tithe, murder,

oppressing the handicapped, failure to care for widows and orphans, deceptive religious pursuits, dishonoring parents, infanticide, witchcraft, and any other iniquity-caused curse.

4.   These curses are now broken back to Adam and Eve and from the actions of every ancestor in between. These curses of biblical abominations are also broken on all future generations. As I break these curses and renounce these abominations, I am once again accepted into fellowship with God and need no longer to feel ashamed to enter His presence.

WHERE TO GET HELP

AUTHOR, PASTOR, RADIO AND TV HOST

The world's foremost expert on cults, the occult, and supernatural phenomena.

PERSONAL TIME WITH BOB LARSON

Are you depressed? Lacking direction in life?
Struggling with relationships? Suffering financial lack or ill health?

LEARN THE KEYS TO SPIRITUAL SUCCESS!

To arrange for your personal, one-on-one spiritual encounter with Bob, email him at Bob@BobLarson.org or call 303-908-1511.

Bob Larson's resources are available online. Let Bob's DVDs, books, and other materials help you on your journey to spiritual freedom.

Go to www.DemonTest.com to discover your level of spiritual need.
Visit all of our web sites listed below:

www.BobLarson.org
www.DemonTest.com
www.TheRealExorcist.com

Curse Breaking

Follow Bob Larson on various social networks. Go to www.BobLarson.org and click on the Blog icon for his daily insights and teaching. To see Bob in action breaking curses and casting out demons, click on his YouTube icon. Don't forget to Like us and Follow us by clicking on the Facebook and Twitter icons.

INTERNATIONAL
SCHOOL OF EXORCISM®
Bob Larson, Founder

MISSION STATEMENT

And when he had called unto him his twelve disciples, he gave them power against unclean spirits, to cast them out!

—MATTHEW 10:1

In an age of increasing evil the ancient spiritual practice of exorcism is in demand. Unfortunately, not a single Protestant denomination has a seminary that teaches exorcism. Those who feel called by God to cast out evil spirits have had nowhere to turn for comprehensive instruction – until now! Rev. Bob Larson, the world's foremost Protestant exorcist, has a vision to restore prayers of exorcism to Christianity and has founded the International School of Exorcism®. Rev. Larson explains, "One-third of all the chapters in the synoptic Gospels contain instances of exorcism and references to demonic possession. In our world of rampant crime, inhumanity, and child abuse, the need to boldly confront demonic forces is more critical than ever."

The School's mission is to train those called to fulfill Christ's command to heal the brokenhearted and set the captives free (Luke 4:18). The curriculum is specifically designed to teach Christian leaders and laypersons the spiritual disciplines of inner healing, deliverance, and exorcism. Various levels of certification are available to those who feel called to this ministry.

Instructional studies include in-depth training in Basic Curse Breaking, the Weapons of Spiritual Warfare, Mental & Emotional Aspects of Deliverance, and Procedures and Principles of Casting out Demons. Applications for enrollment are now being received, but space is limited. Detailed information is available at www.BobLarson.org by clicking on the SCHOOL OF EXORCISM button at the top of the home page.

For more information, please contact the Director of Admissions at:

Bob Larson's International School of Exorcism®
P. O. Box 36480, Denver, Colorado 80236
exorcismschool@boblarson.org
303-980-1511
www.boblarson.org

IN THE RIGHT HANDS, THIS BOOK WILL CHANGE LIVES!

Most of the people who need this message will not be looking for this book. To change their lives, you need to put a copy of this book in their hands.

> *But others (seeds) fell into good ground, and brought forth fruit, some a hundred-fold, some sixty-fold, some thirty-fold* (Matthew 13:8).

Our ministry is constantly seeking methods to find the good ground, the people who need this anointed message to change their lives. Will you help us reach these people?

> *Remember this—a farmer who plants only a few seeds will get a small crop. But the one who plants generously will get a generous crop* (2 Corinthians 9:6).

EXTEND THIS MINISTRY BY SOWING
3 BOOKS, 5 BOOKS, 10 BOOKS, OR MORE TODAY,
AND BECOME A LIFE CHANGER!

Thank you,

Don Nori Sr., Founder
Destiny Image
Since 1982